Date:

This book belongs to:

THINGS YOU WANTED TO SAY BUT NEVER DID

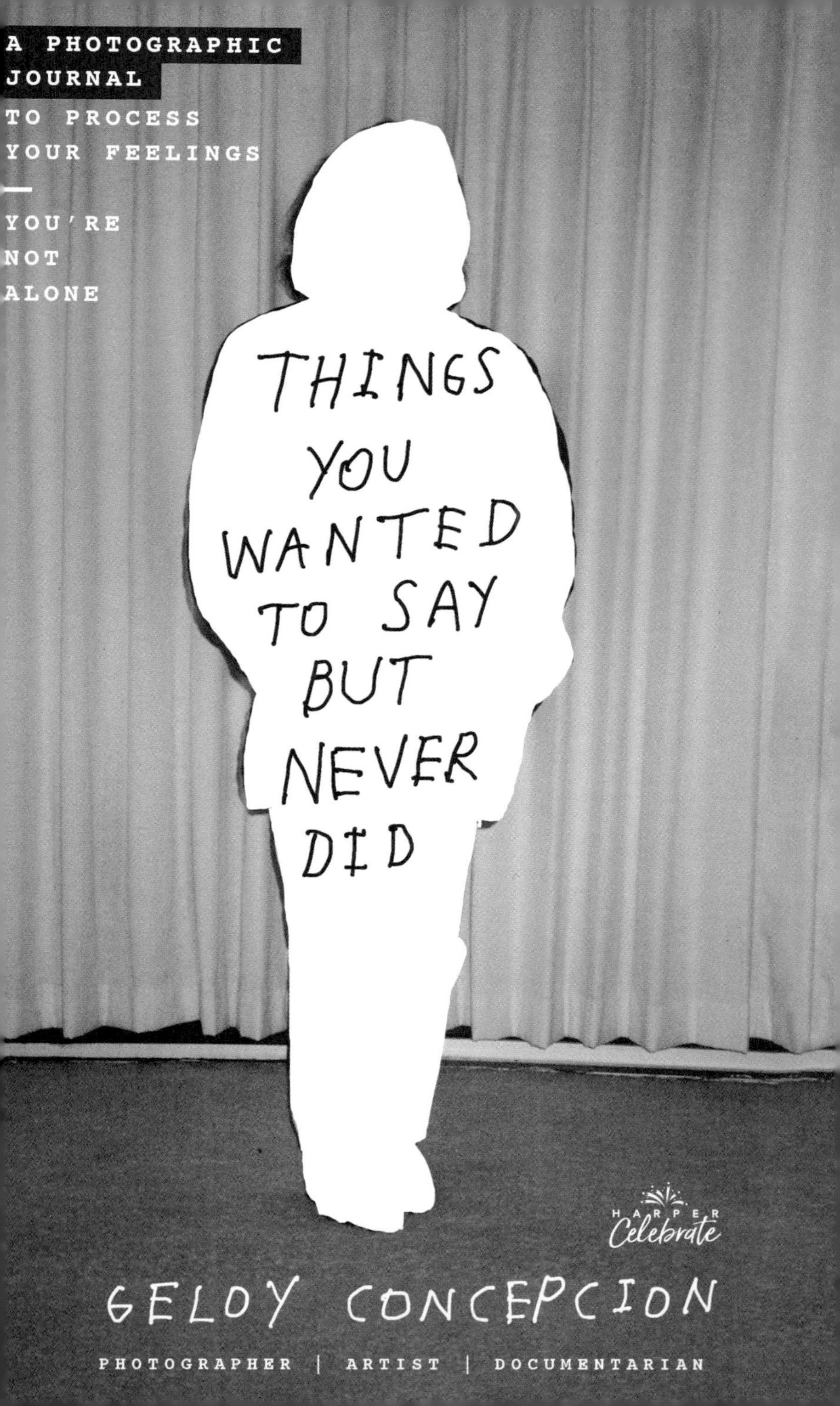
A PHOTOGRAPHIC JOURNAL
TO PROCESS YOUR FEELINGS
—
YOU'RE NOT ALONE
THINGS YOU WANTED TO SAY BUT NEVER DID
HARPER Celebrate
GELOY CONCEPCION
PHOTOGRAPHER | ARTIST | DOCUMENTARIAN

Things You Wanted to Say But Never Did

Published by Harper Celebrate, an imprint of HarperCollins Focus LLC.

Note: This publication is meant to encourage reflection and introspection as a source of valuable experience for the reader. However, it is not meant as a substitute for professional or expert assistance with one's mental health and well-being. If such level of assistance is required, the services of a competent professional should be sought. This book is only for informational and educational purposes and should not be considered therapy or any form of treatment. If you think you need assistance, call your local emergency number or the mental health crisis hotline listed in your local government pages. Or visit www.mentalhealth.gov for additional resources.

ISBN 978-1-4002-3895-8 (TP)

Printed in India

26 27 REP 6 5

This book is dedicated to my
family, Liberty and Narra.
To the community of strangers, friends I've
never met, who trusted me with their stories
and let me share them with the world.
To you, my dear reader.

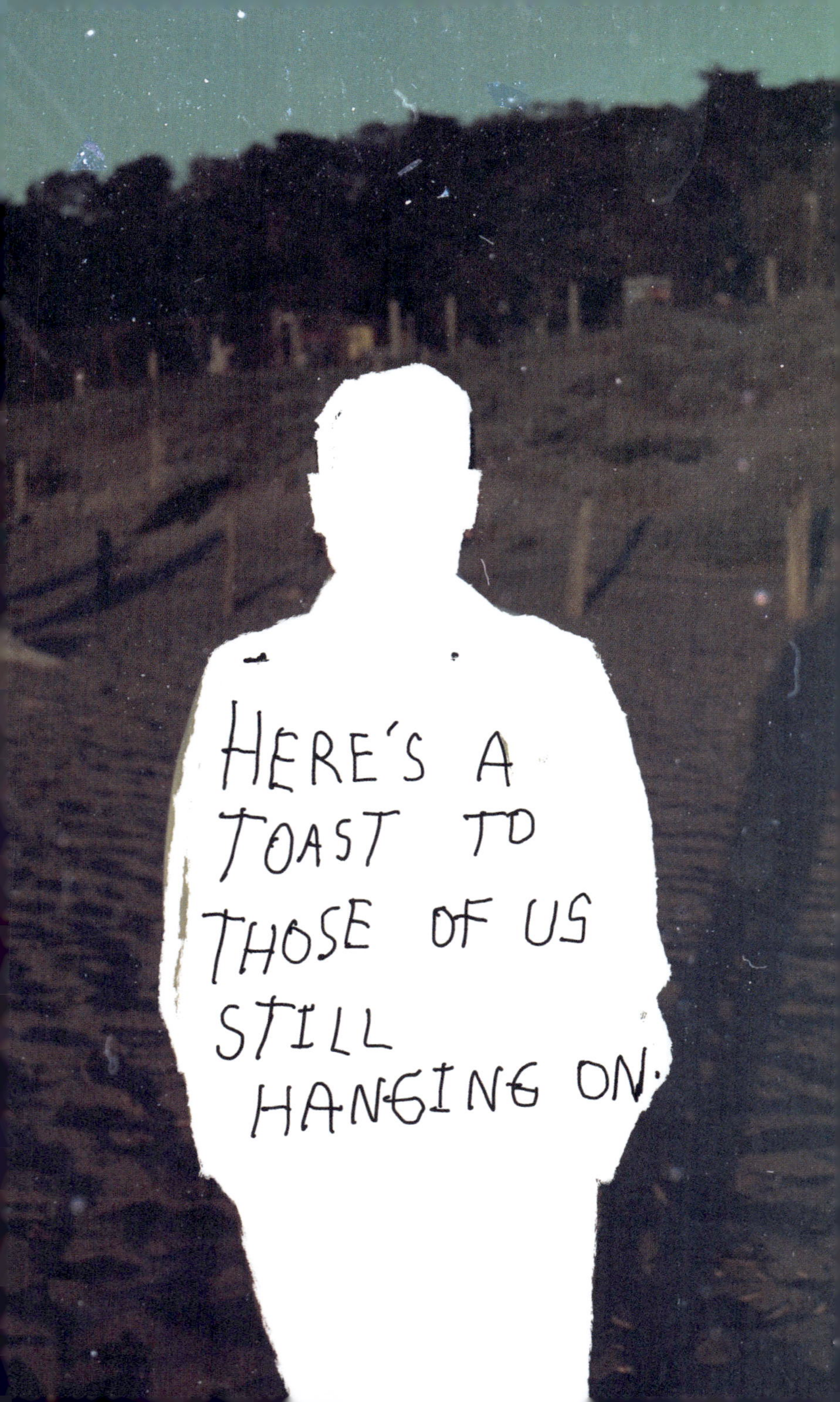
HERE'S A
TOAST TO
THOSE OF US
STILL
HANGING ON.

INTRODUCTION

It all began in 2019, two years after I arrived in the United States from the Philippines. I couldn't work due to some delays on my immigration papers, I was a new father who couldn't seem to find a way to provide for his family, I was feeling lost, and I was about to quit photography. I had all these concerns swirling in my mind.

I figured I couldn't be the only one going through a difficult time, so I turned to Instagram and asked people, "What are the things you wanted to say but never did?"

And that's how it all began.

I started this project to provide a safe space for these answers—for everything we find painful to confront when we're alone. Things we want to voice out loud but can't for some reason. Maybe because we lack the courage, or we're afraid we'll sound crazy, or we might hurt someone's feelings. Maybe because it's too late.

So, my Instagram account became a place where people could share the things they couldn't say before, with the hope that maybe somewhere out there, someone else going through something similar could see their thoughts and feel some sense of relief that they're not alone. We all live different lives, but these shared experiences bond us. The road might seem too dark and lonely, but please remember you're not alone.

We walk together.

This project will keep on going until the last note is received.

—Geloy

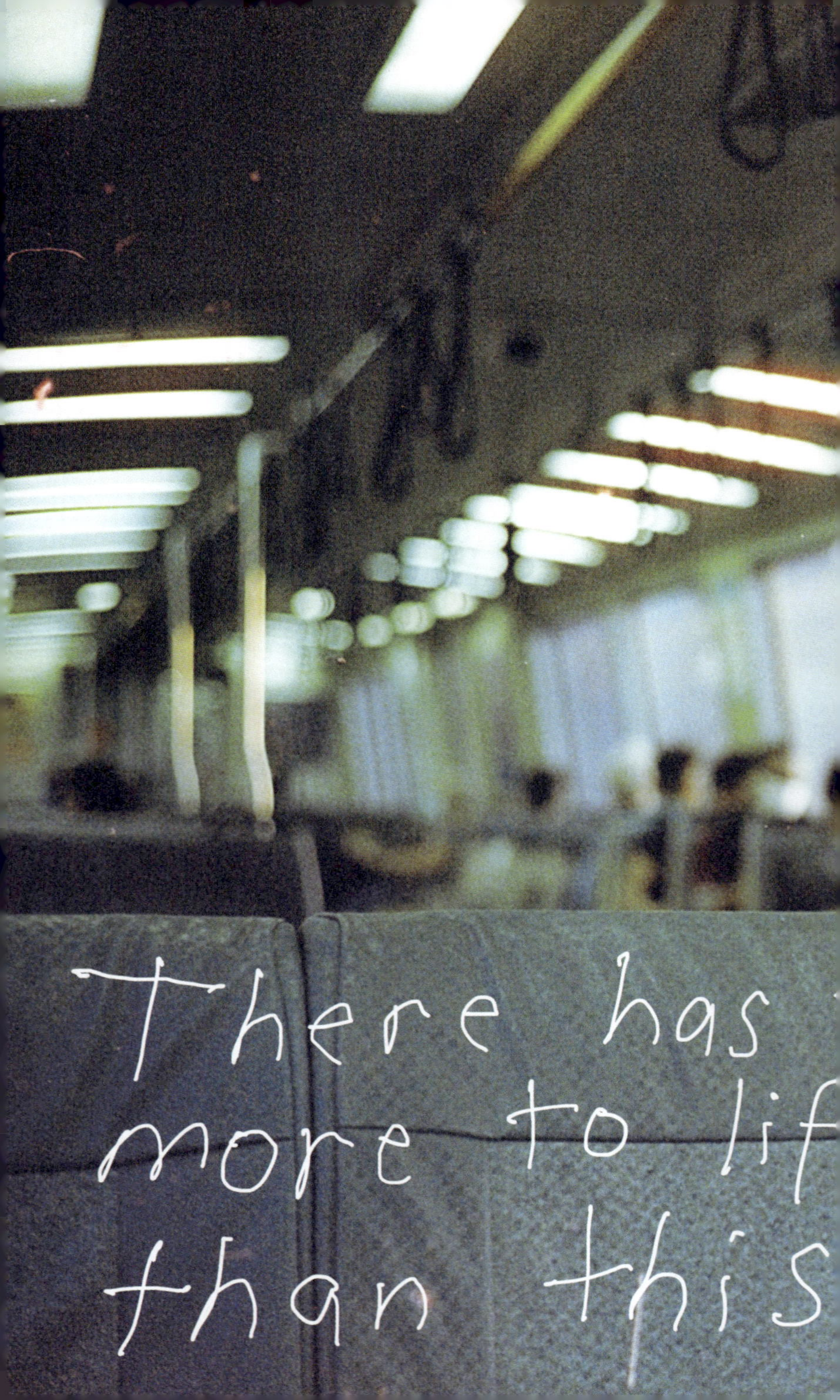
There has
more to lif
than this

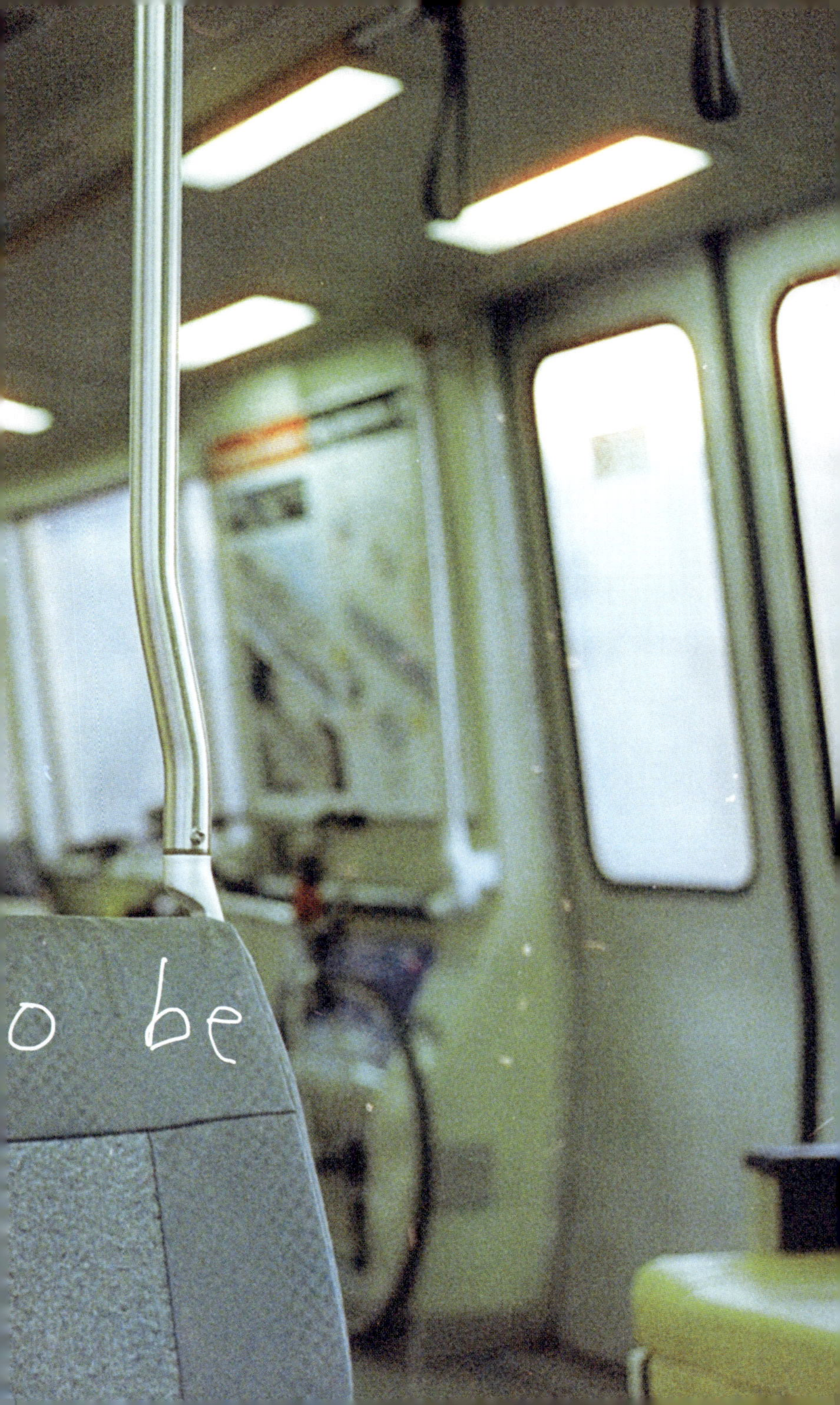
o be

“You are here for a reason.”

—GELOY CONCEPCION

A NOTE TO THE READER

There is no perfect way to process your emotional experiences, but this journal is a tool to help you through the journey. You can write on every page, or none of them. You can keep this as a unified book, or tear out pages to frame or give to other people.

Like the story of your life, *Things You Wanted to Say But Never Did* is a project comprised of genuine emotions commonly felt among all people—joy, sadness, longing, redemption—but experienced in a way that is unique to you.

The most important thing to remember is that you are not alone, and even on the darkest of days, there is always light waiting to be found. These pages are an invitation to spend some time with yourself—to forgive, to heal, to hope—and to connect with others.

You are here for a reason.

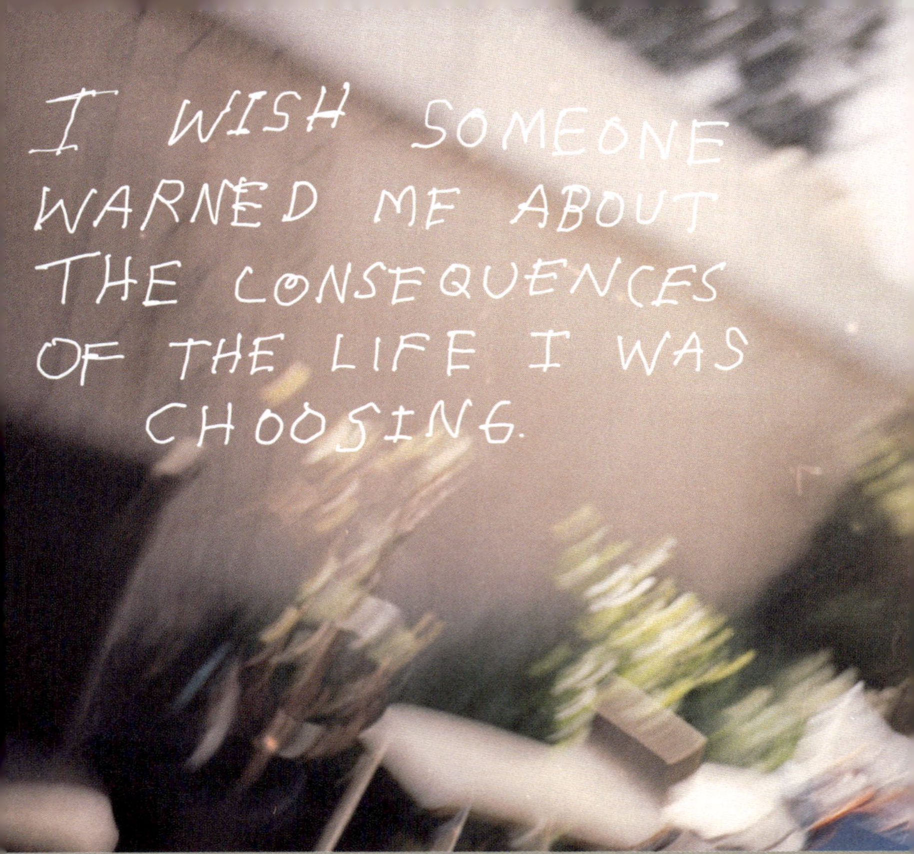

Is the life you lead a result of the choices you've made, or are the choices you've made a result of the life you've led? Do you have free will, or has everything been determined for you? Either way, if someone had warned you about what was to come, would you have made different decisions?

"All saints have past and
all sinners have a future."

Anton Chekhov

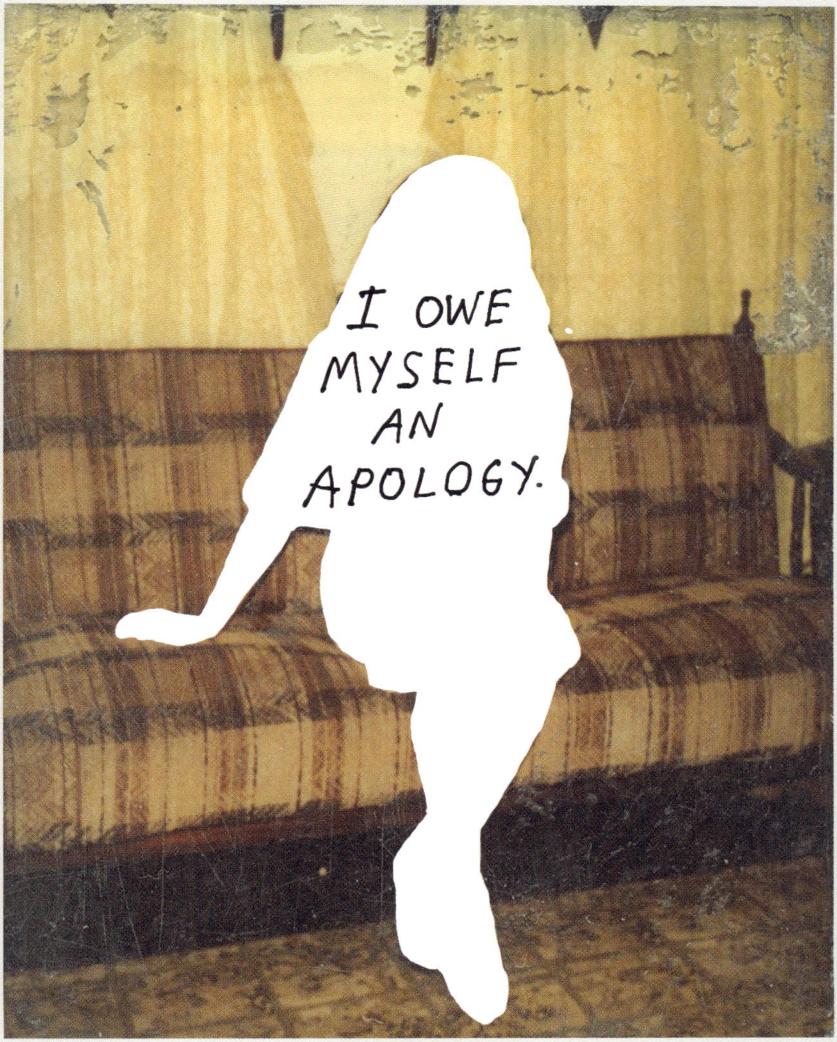
I OWE
MYSELF
AN
APOLOGY.

Some of the deepest wounds are the ones we inflict on ourselves. Imagine you could go back in time to meet a younger version of yourself. What would you apologize for? You are worthy of forgiveness; it's time to make amends.

"I am no bird; and no net ensnares me; I am a free human being with an independent will . . ."

Charlotte Brontë

Sometimes one single action can have long-lasting, even life-changing, consequences. Return in time to the point of your trauma, or any significant event from your past. Now, travel from that moment to an alternative future that might exist if things had happened differently. Who else have you become in this other timeline?

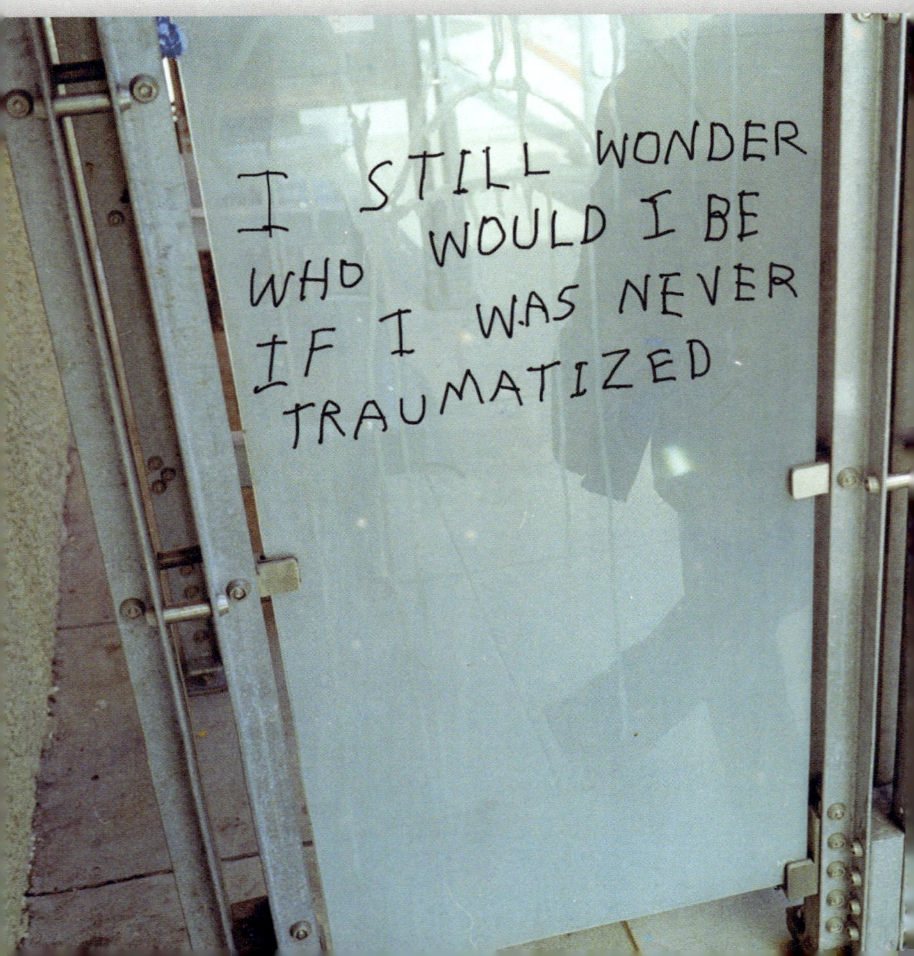

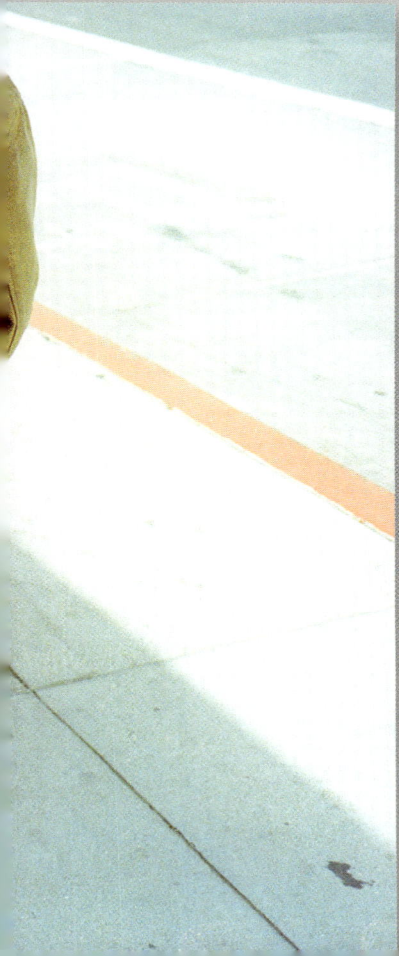

"The wound is the
place where the
Light enters you."
Rumi

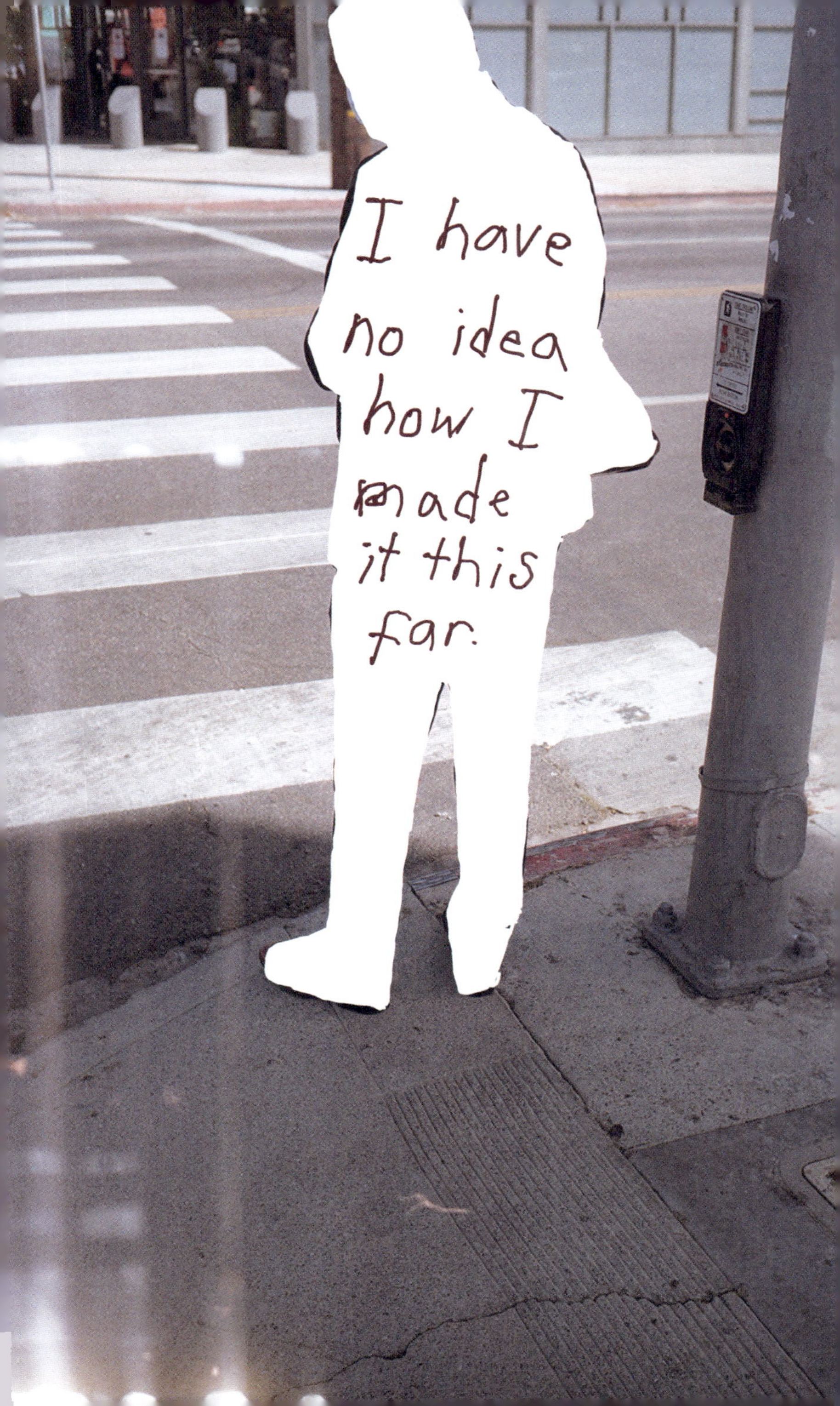
I have
no idea
how I
made
it this
far.

Imagine your life—past, present, and future—as if it's a journey through the woods. Some paths are clear and brightly lit, while others are covered in shadows, leaving you unable to see your next step forward. Which paths in your life have been the easy ones to travel, and which ones have been treacherous? How has traveling both pathways equipped you for the ones ahead?

"If you do not change direction, you may end up where you are heading."

Lao Tzu

There is a difference between selfishness and self-care. In order to take care of anyone, we must be able to take proper care of ourselves. What are some small ways you can fill your cup today? How will that energize you to be more fully present for the people in your life?

FOR ONCE IN
MY LIFE
I WANT TO
BE A LITTLE
SELFISH.

"Have patience
with all things,
but chiefly have
patience with
yourself."
Francis de Sales

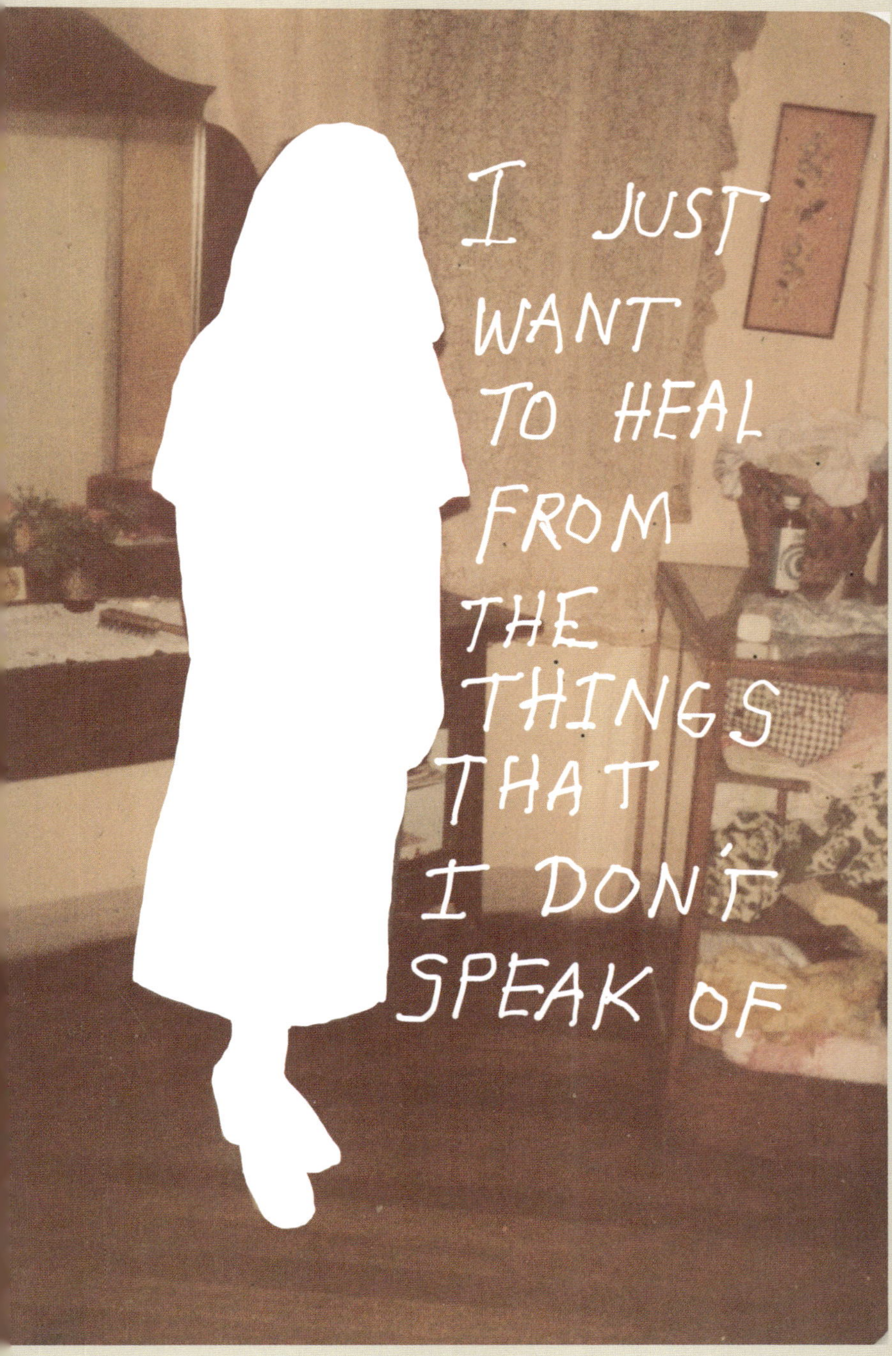
I JUST
WANT
TO HEAL
FROM
THE
THINGS
THAT
I DON'T
SPEAK OF

The poet Walt Whitman suggests that in order to heal, you should sing a song of yourself. If you'd rather not sing, at least try composing a song about the things you don't speak of. Try rhyming if you need help to get started.

"I too am not a bit tamed,
I too am untranslatable,
I sound my barbaric yawp
over the roofs of the world."
Walt Whitman

By the time he was fourteen, Andre the Giant was seven feet, four inches tall. After growing so fast, and in order to survive and thrive, he became known as the gentlest person in professional wrestling.

How did *you* overcome your biological or environmental difficulties?

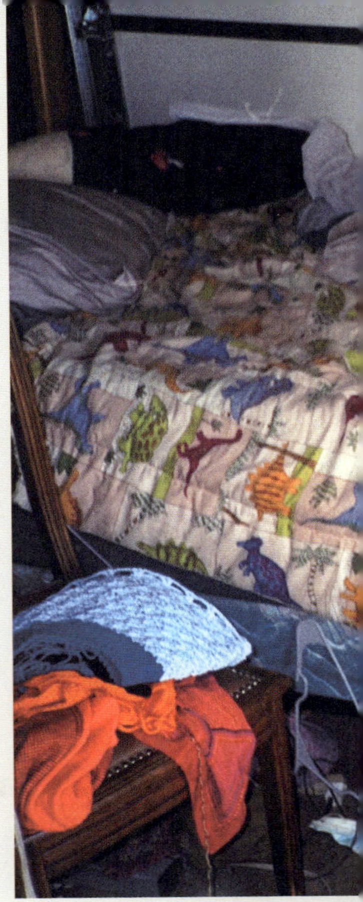

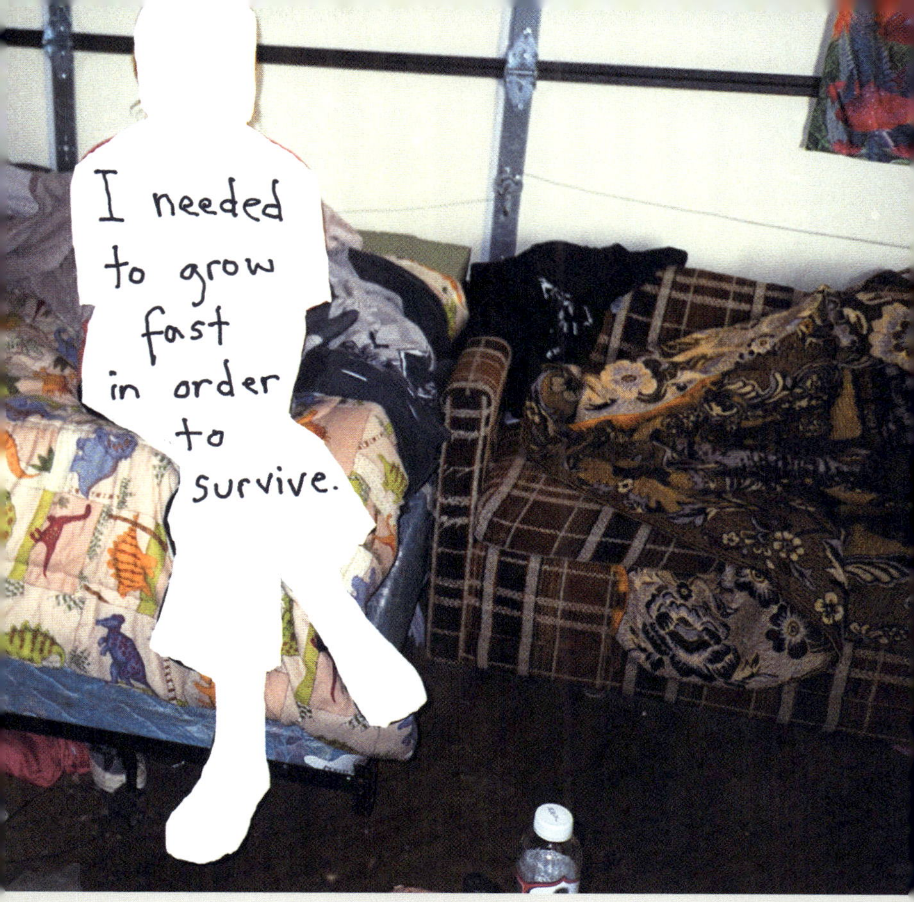
I needed
to grow
fast
in order
to
survive.

"Out of your
vulnerabilities
will come your
strength."
Sigmund Freud

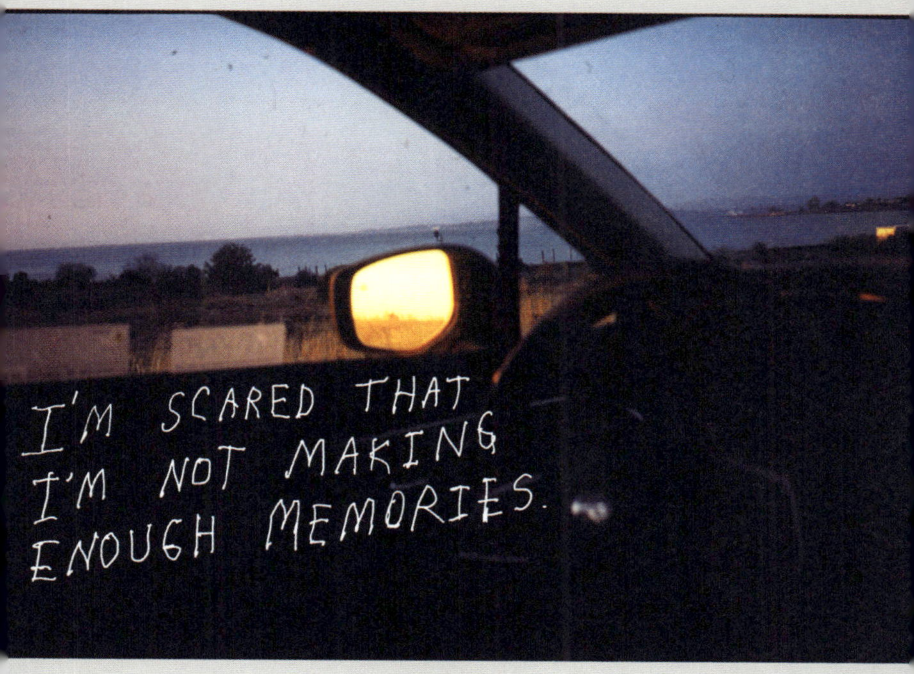
I'M SCARED THAT
I'M NOT MAKING
ENOUGH MEMORIES.

A memory is the way an event is encoded in your mind. So your brain does quite literally "make" your memories. Are you worried that you're not having enough meaningful experiences? Or is it that your mind isn't encoding the experiences in a way that makes them feel like they matter?

This evening, write down at least three small things that happened today that made you feel grateful. Does looking at the seemingly forgettable parts of your day with this new perspective make them feel more meaningful and memorable?

"Cultivate the habit of being grateful for every good thing that comes to you, and to give thanks continuously."

Ralph Waldo Emerson

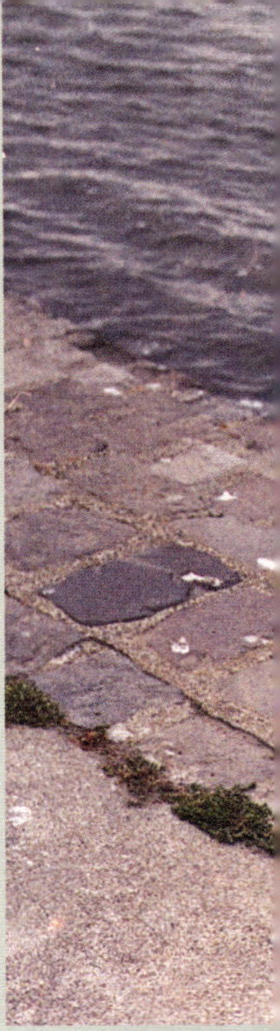

When we look back on our happiest memories, they can often appear as if they're sepia-toned, still frames from our favorite movie. What if you looked at the present through the same lens?

Go through an entire day as if it's a collection of scenes from a film. You are the screenwriter, director, and lead actor. At the end of the day, transcribe your favorite scene. Are you writing it the way it actually happened, or the way you remember it? Which outcome matters more?

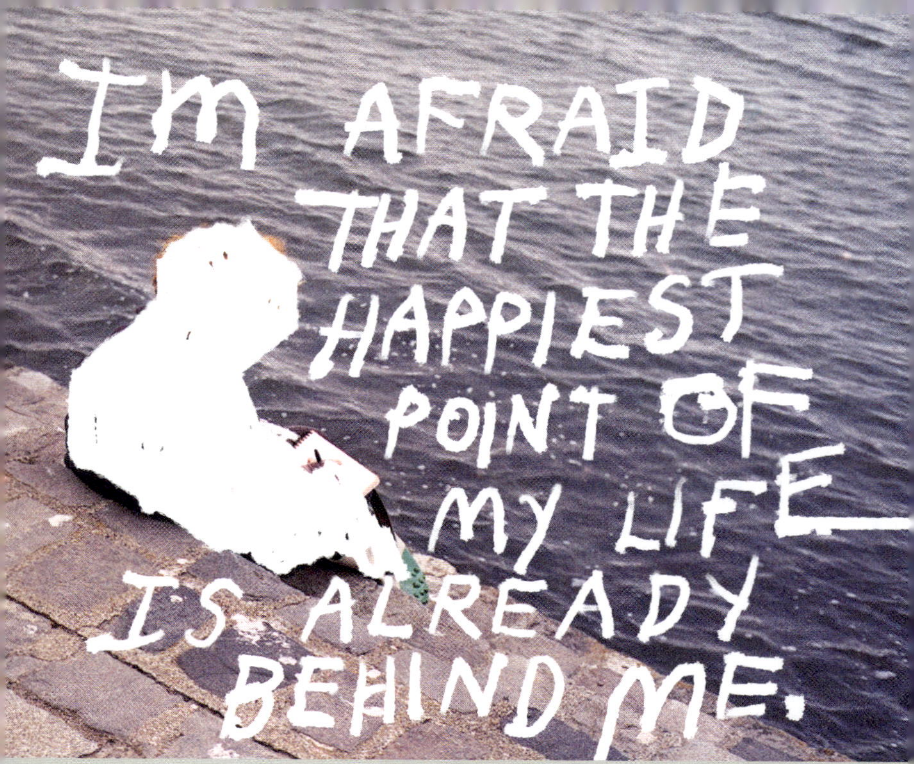
I'M AFRAID
THAT THE
HAPPIEST
POINT OF
MY LIFE
IS ALREADY
BEHIND ME.

"There is something
in us, as storytellers
and as listeners to
stories, that demands
the redemptive act,
that demands that
what falls at least
be offered the chance
to be restored."

Flannery O'Connor

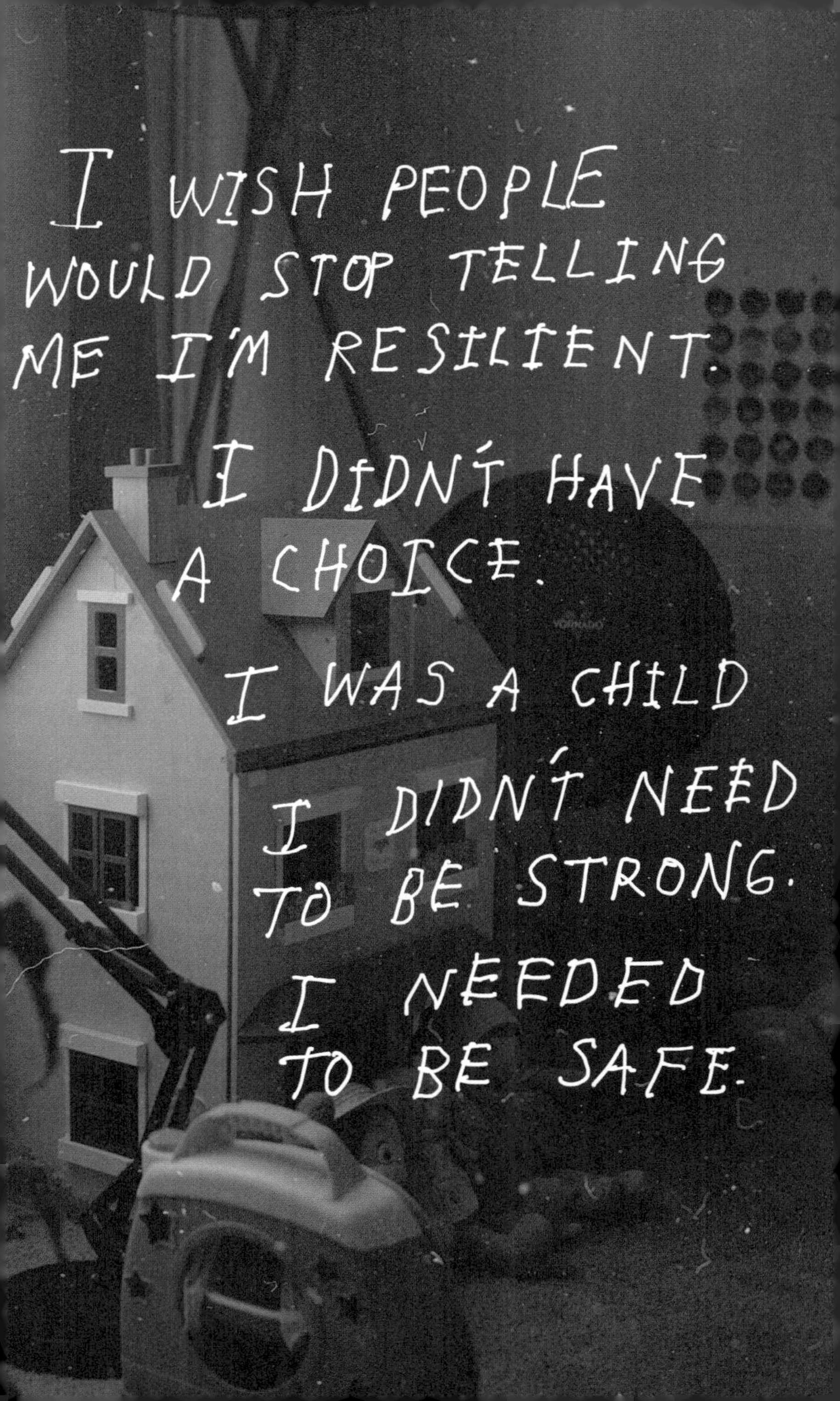
I WISH PEOPLE
WOULD STOP TELLING
ME I'M RESILIENT.
I DIDN'T HAVE
A CHOICE.
I WAS A CHILD
I DIDN'T NEED
TO BE STRONG.
I NEEDED
TO BE SAFE.

People use buzzwords as shortcuts to avoid truly engaging with each other's emotional experiences. Reflect on a time when you felt unheard, and write about how you would have preferred your listener to have responded.

"You heard me cry long before I knew my voice."

A. D. Posey

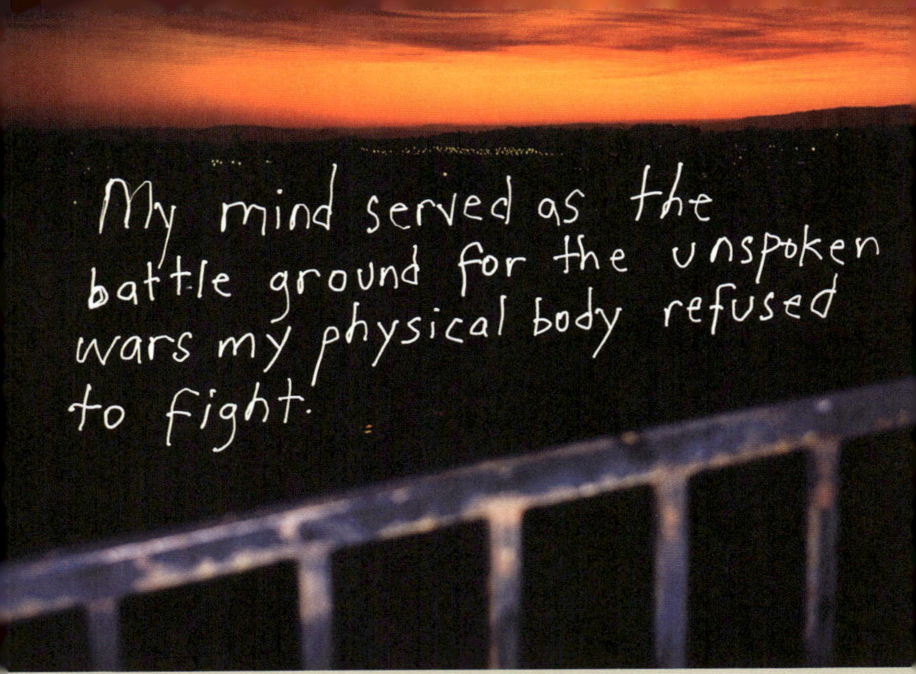

Sometimes the traumas inflicted on our physical bodies can have consequences felt in our emotional or mental state. Likewise, stress, anxiety, and sadness can often have impacts felt in our bodies.

Have you ever experienced this? Try engaging in a physical activity—take a walk, go for a swim, build something with your hands, or even lie down for a nap—and see if it has an impact on how you feel emotionally.

"The supreme art of war
is to subdue the enemy
without fighting."

Sun Tzu

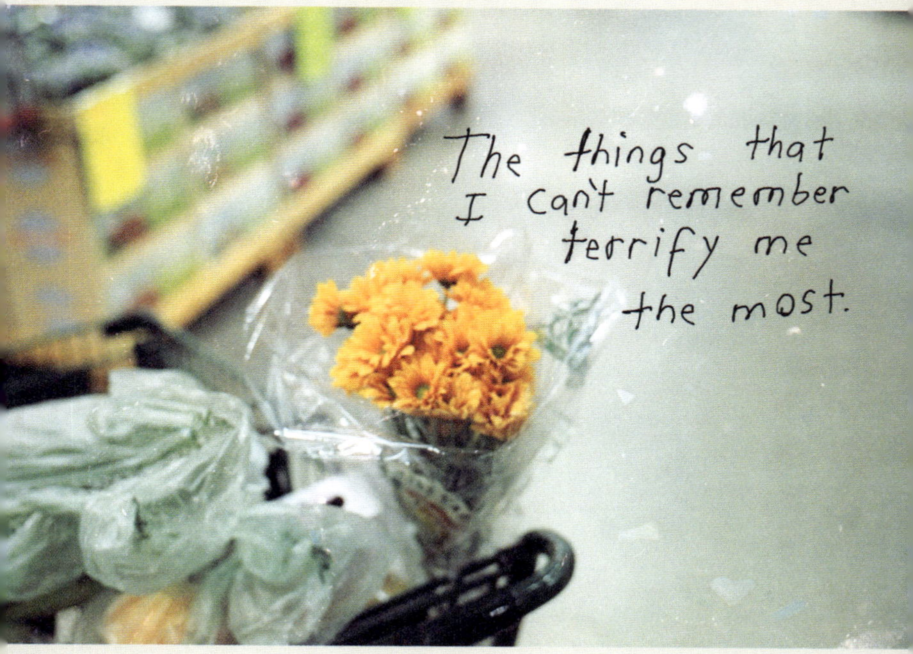
The things that
I can't remember
terrify me
the most.

Which frightens you more: the things you remember that you wish to forget, or the fear that you won't be able to remember those things at all?

"If you wish to forget anything on the spot, make a note that this thing is to be remembered."

Edgar Allan Poe

Is it possible for anyone to feel like they fit in anywhere without feeling like they fit in with themselves first? Describe what might make you feel more comfortable with yourself before your next birthday.

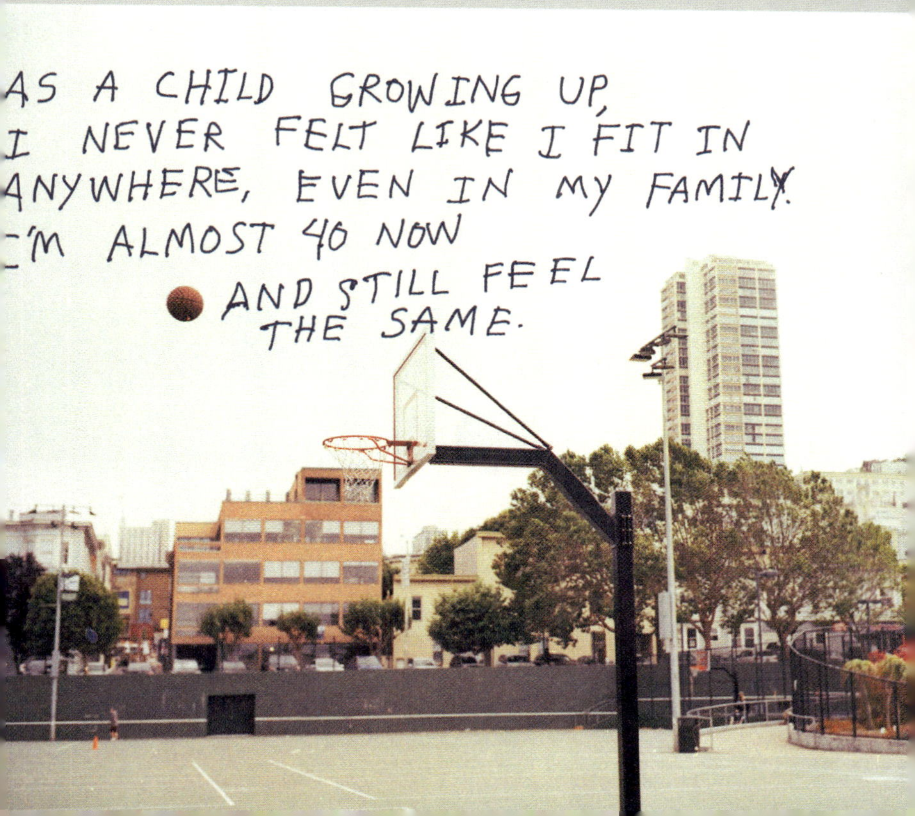
AS A CHILD GROWING UP,
I NEVER FELT LIKE I FIT IN
ANYWHERE, EVEN IN MY FAMILY.
I'M ALMOST 40 NOW
AND STILL FEEL
THE SAME.

"I am not what happened to me, I am what I choose to become."

Carl Jung

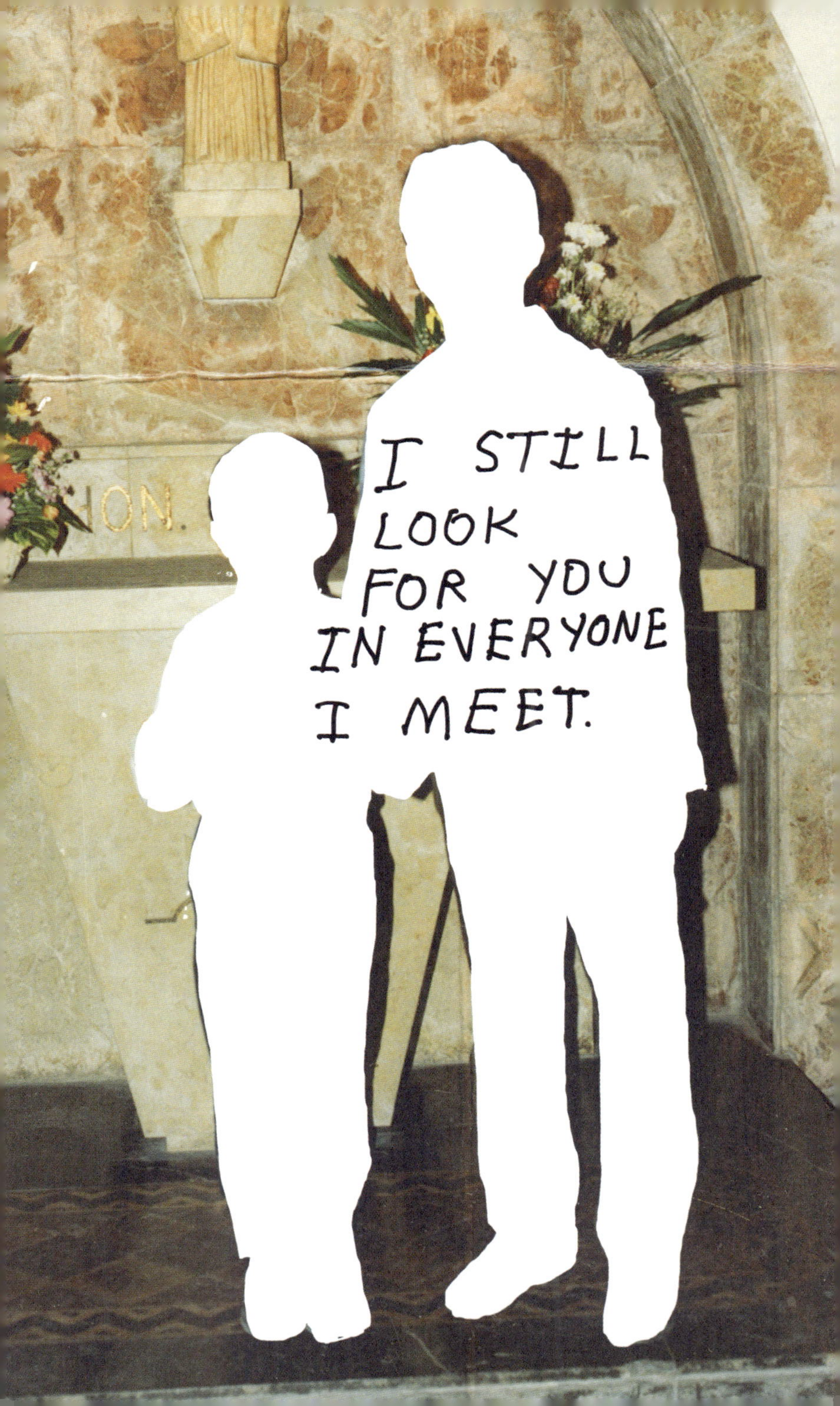
HON.
I STILL
LOOK
FOR YOU
IN EVERYONE
I MEET.

Is there someone in your past who has kept you from going forward into the future? Write a letter to that person to thank them for playing a part in your life, and then let them know it's time for you to take their contribution and move on.

"As you get older,
it's more difficult
to have heroes,
but it is sort
of necessary."
Ernest Hemingway

Imposter! *Fraud! Phony!*

I'm not as smart as they think I am.

I don't deserve my success; I'm barely keeping it together.

What happens when they see under the mask I'm wearing?

Describe the mask that you wear and how it differs from the face that you believe hides behind it.

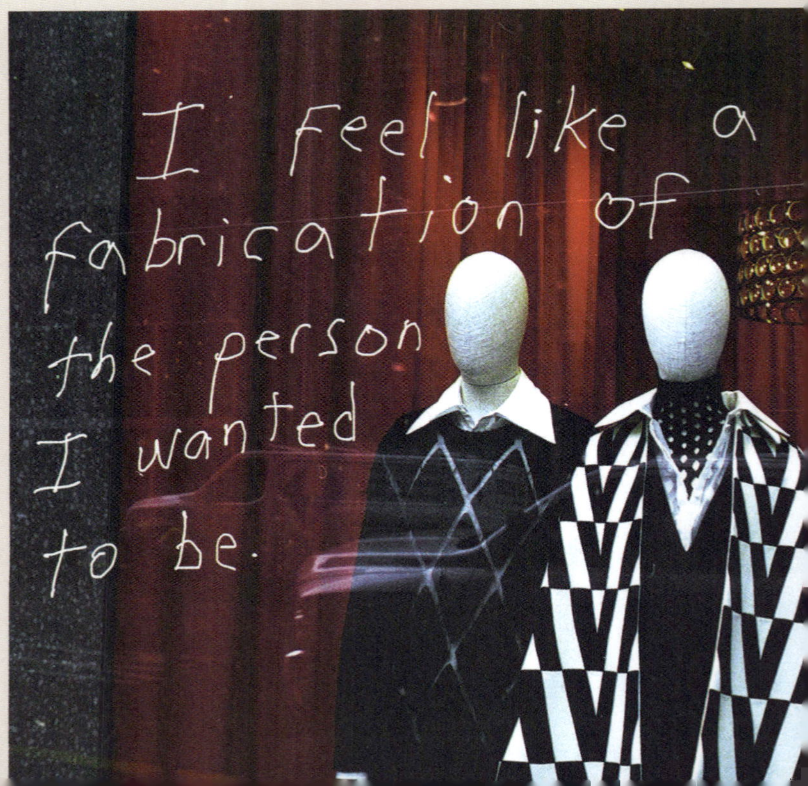

"No man, for any
considerable period, can
wear one face to himself and
another to the multitude,
without finally getting
bewildered as to which
may be the true."

Nathaniel Hawthorne

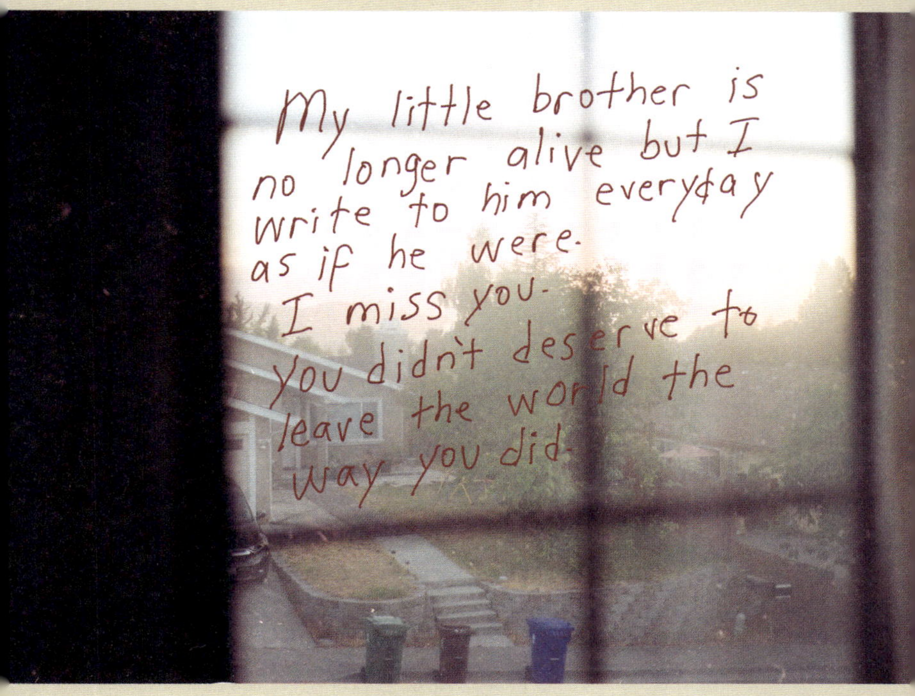
My little brother is
no longer alive but I
write to him everyday
as if he were.
I miss you.
You didn't deserve to
leave the world the
way you did.

When writing to people who have passed away, either on the page or in our hearts and minds, we tend to communicate with the person they were when they passed. However, over time, *we* continue to grow and change. Write to someone you've lost, but write to the person they'd be *now* rather than the person they were when you knew them.

"Where you used to be, there is a hole in the world, which I find myself constantly walking around in the daytime, and falling in at night. I miss you like hell."

Edna St. Vincent Millay

Someone once said, "It feels like the world is only made for the brave."

Or is bravery made only by having to live in the world?

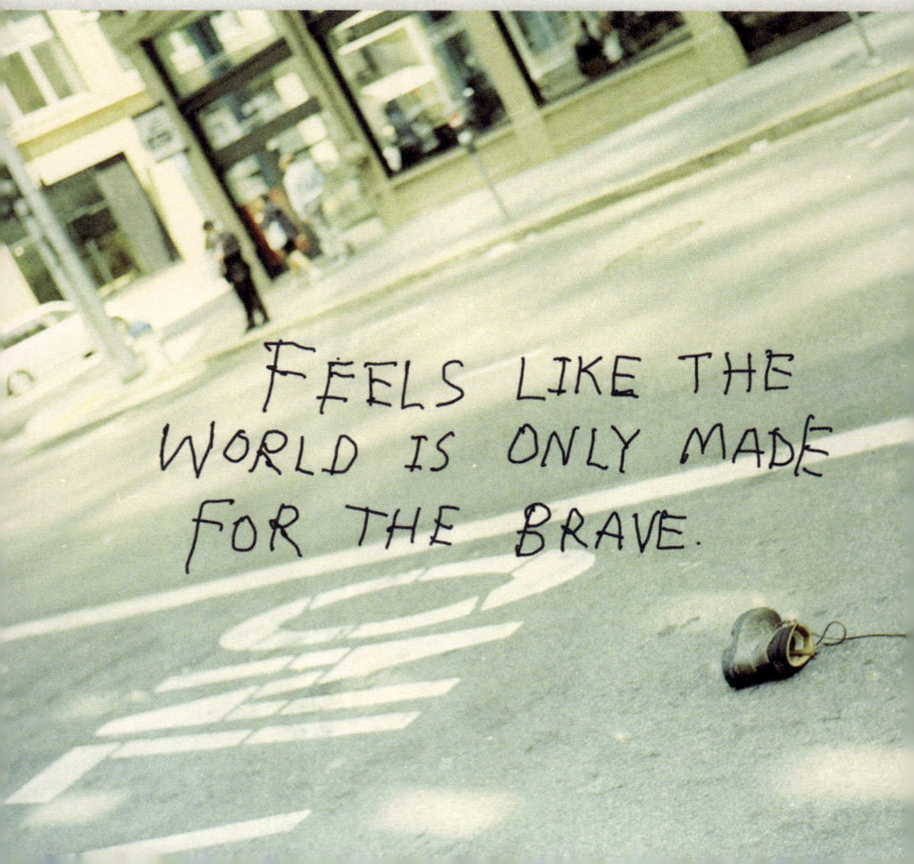

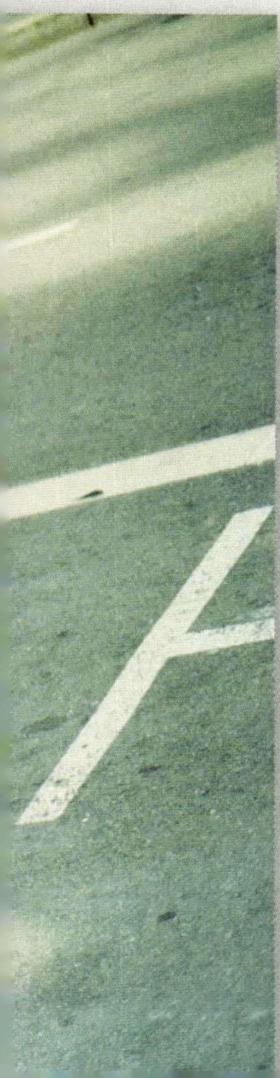

"Courage is found in
unlikely places."
J. R. R. Tolkien

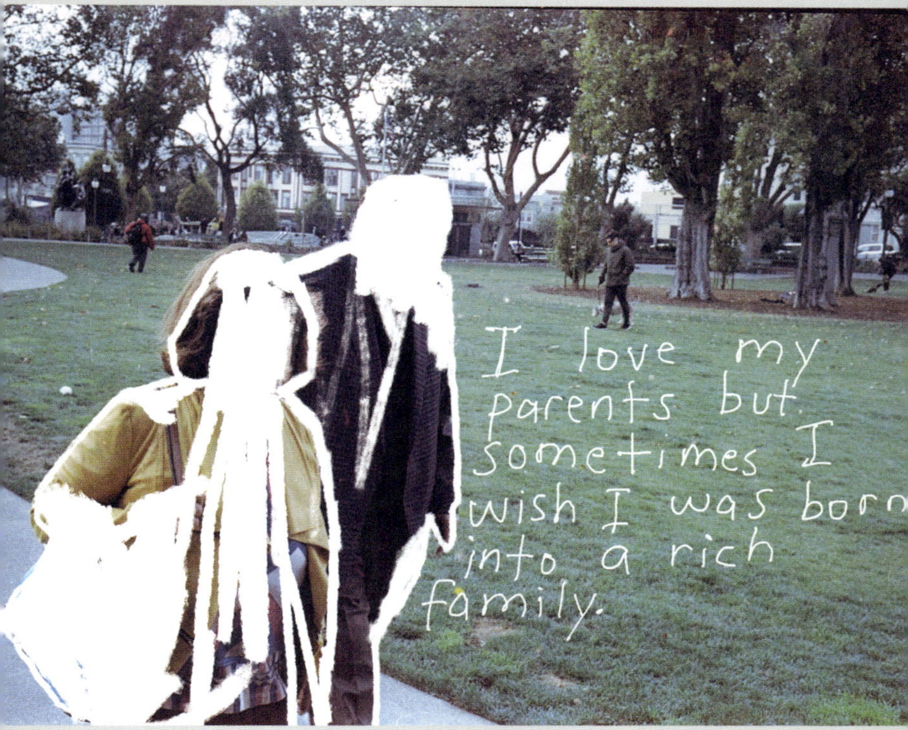
I love my parents but sometimes I wish I was born into a rich family.

What if wealth and love were mutually exclusive? A zero-sum game. Imagine a long life with plentiful riches but no affection. Describe how that might feel. Now, imagine a life led in poverty, but with devoted family and friends. Be honest: Which life would you choose?

"I'd like to live as a poor man with lots of money."

Pablo Picasso

Is there an area of your life where it feels as if no matter how much effort you put in, it never seems to be enough? On the other hand, are there things that have come easily to you with little to no labor on your end? Which brings you more contentment?

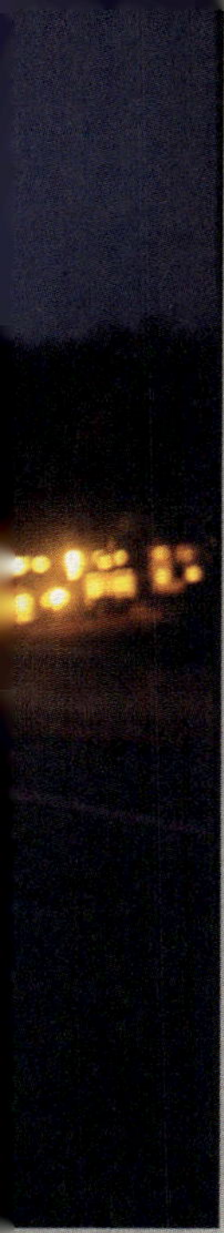

"Real generosity to the
future lies in giving
all to the present."

Albert Camus

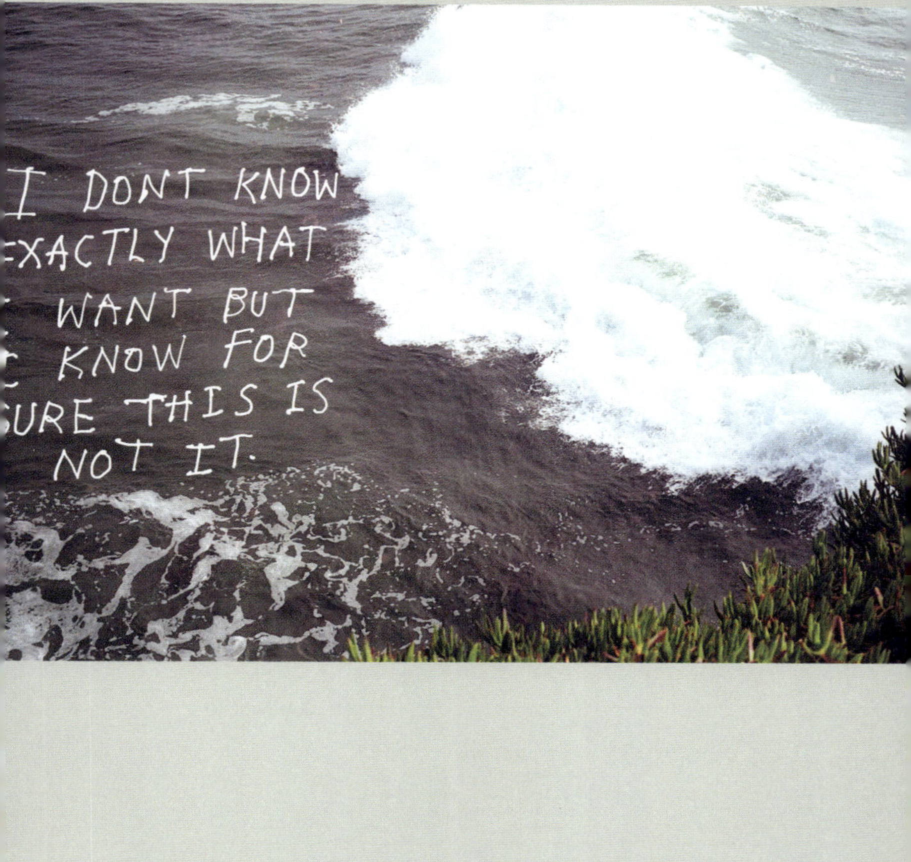
I DONT KNOW
XACTLY WHAT
WANT BUT
KNOW FOR
URE THIS IS
NOT IT.

Is it better to know what you want and not be able to have it, or to be dissatisfied with what you have but unable to define what you want?

"I prefer to be a dreamer among the humblest, with visions to be realized, than lord among those without dreams and desires."

Khalil Gibran

The ancient Greeks had many definitions for the modern English word *love*.

Agape is delight in the object of love.

Eros is sexual passion.

Philia is loyalty to friends.

The importance of each changes as we age. How have you noticed this change progress over the course of your life? Which type is most important to you now?

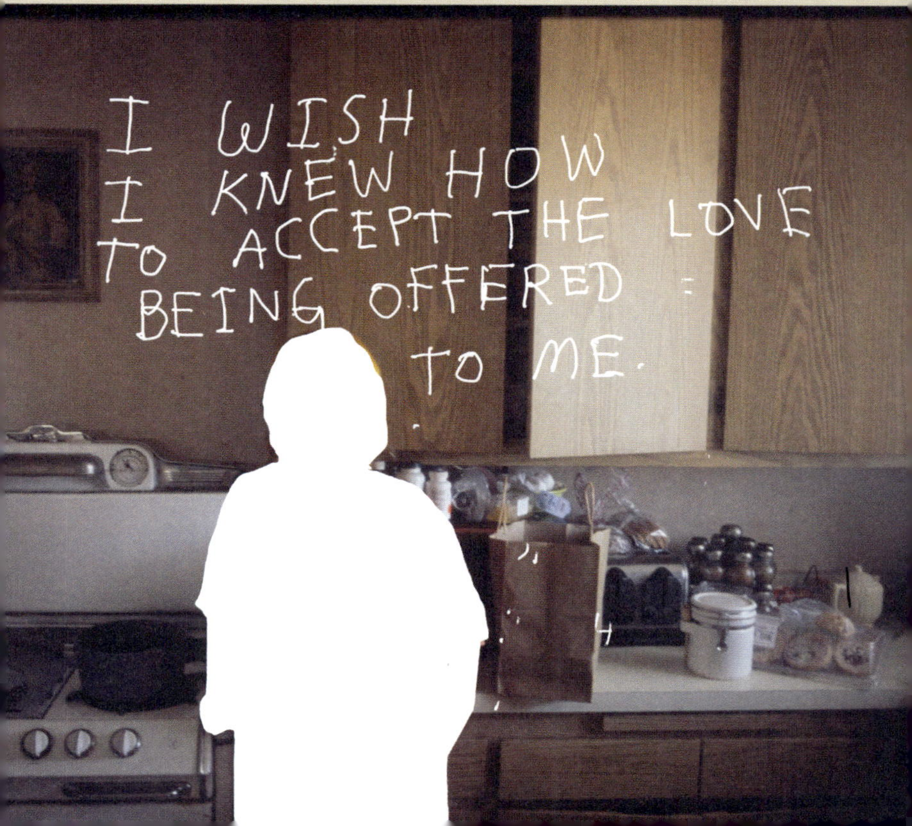
I WISH
I KNEW HOW
TO ACCEPT THE LOVE
BEING OFFERED
TO ME.

"Seize the moments of
happiness, love and be loved!
That is the only reality
in the world, all else is
folly. It is the one thing we
are interested in here."

Leo Tolstoy

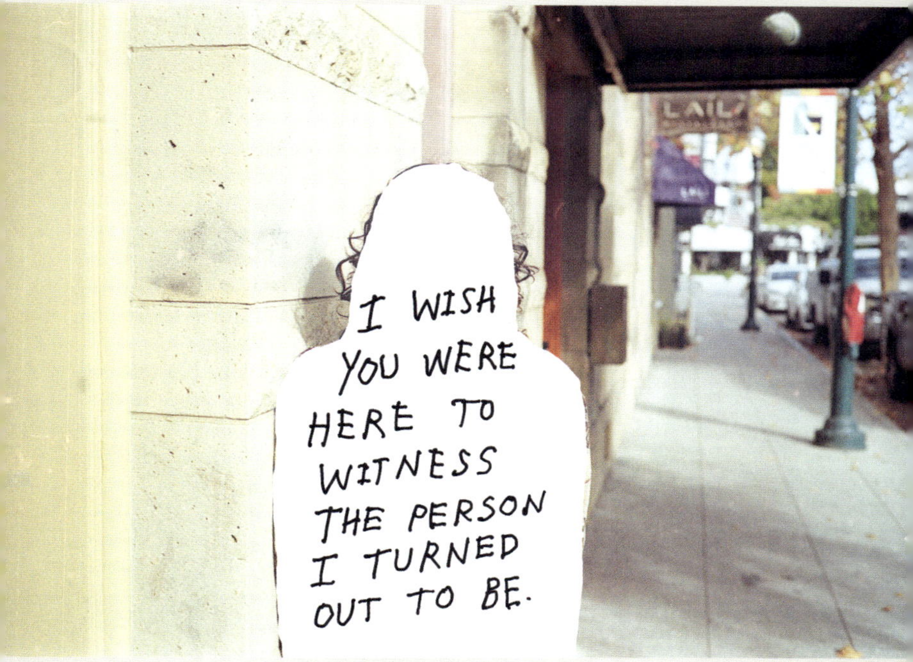
I WISH
YOU WERE
HERE TO
WITNESS
THE PERSON
I TURNED
OUT TO BE.

Look back at your life and consider to what degree being watched by others has contributed to who you've become. Have the effects of this been mostly positive, negative, or perhaps a mix of both?

"Strange feeling that someone is looking at me. I am clear, then dim, then gone, then dim again, then clear again, and so on, back and forth, in and out of someone's eye."

Samuel Beckett

Think of a time when you sacrificed your own happiness in order to achieve a goal. Or sacrificed something for the benefit of someone else's good. Looking back, do you regret this decision, or do you still believe you made the right choice?

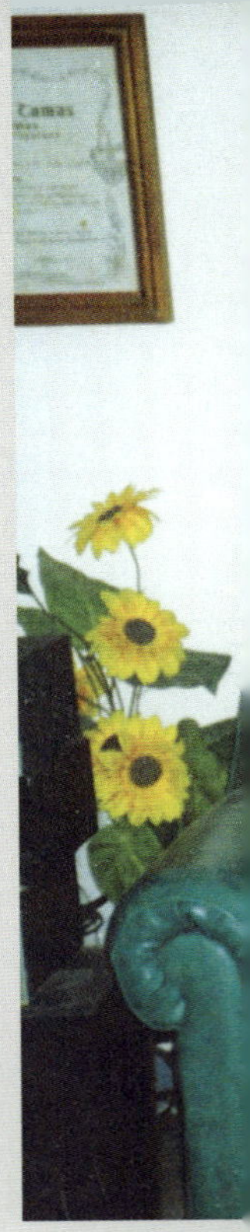

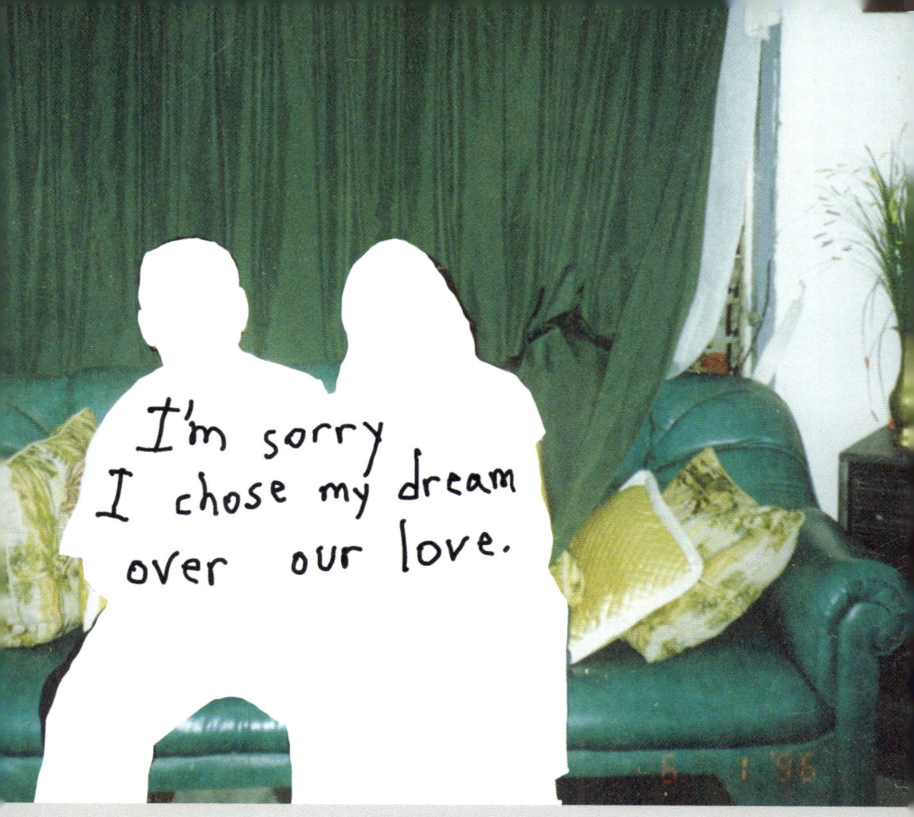
I'm sorry
I chose my dream
over our love.
6 1 '96

"Hold fast to dreams
For if dreams die
Life is a broken-winged bird
That cannot fly."
Langston Hughes

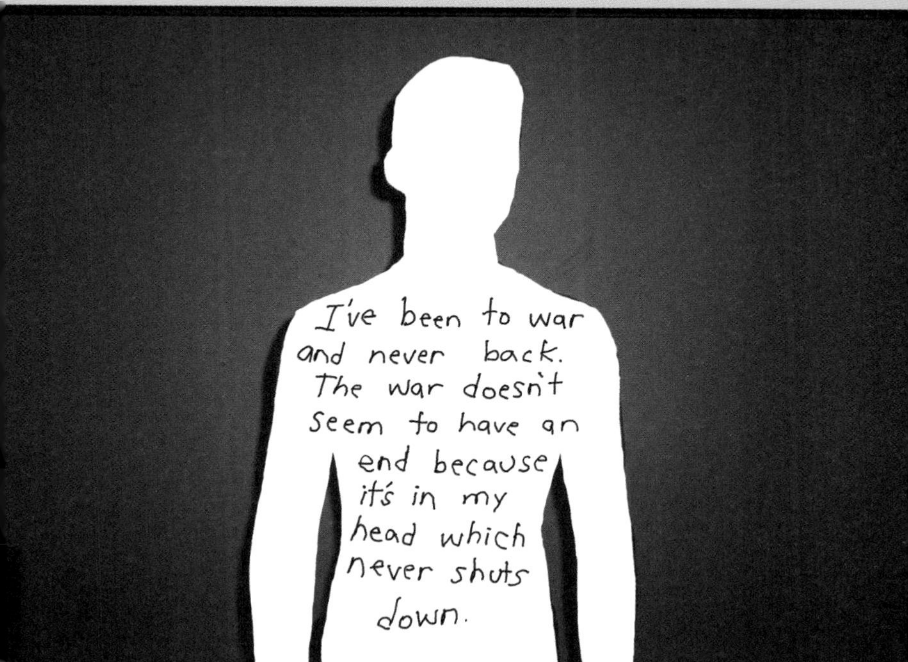
I've been to war
and never back.
The war doesn't
seem to have an
end because
it's in my
head which
never shuts
down.

I**n severe cases** of post-traumatic stress disorder (PTSD), a traumatic event is often relived in a person's head endlessly and feels just as real as the actual occurrence itself.

Have you ever had an experience that plays on repeat in your mind? Were you able to break the time loop? How? If not, spend some time reflecting on all that's happened in your life between the moment of your trauma and the present. Where do you want to go from here?

You have the power to choose.

"Everything can be taken from a man but one thing: the last of the human freedoms—to choose one's attitude in any given set of circumstances, to choose one's own way."

Viktor Frankl

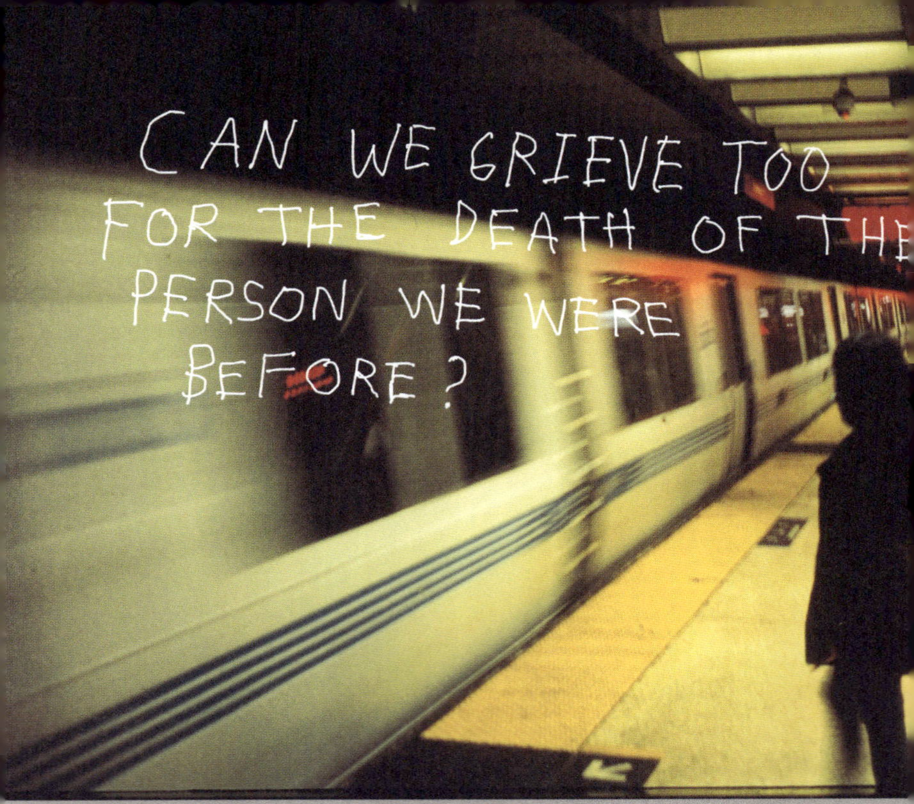

Tomorrow, you are going to attend the funeral of the person you once were. Write a eulogy for your former self, then find a token that represents them. Give your speech, and bury the token in the ground.

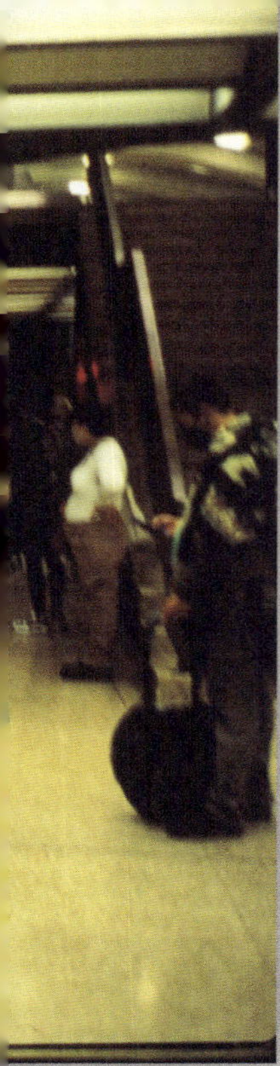

"I demolish my bridges behind me . . . then there is no choice but to move forward."

Fridtjof Nansen

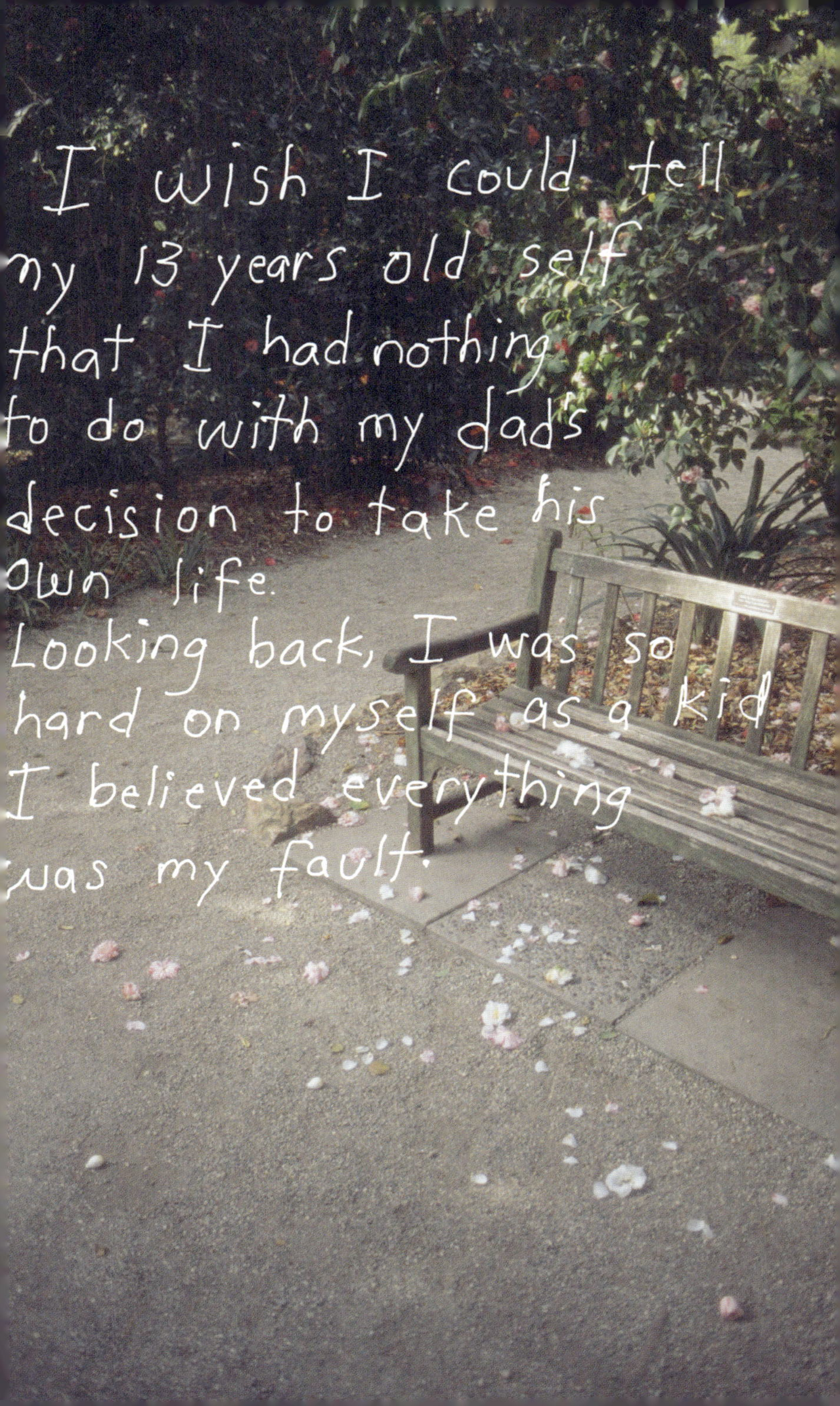
I wish I could tell
my 13 years old self
that I had nothing
to do with my dad's
decision to take his
own life.
Looking back, I was so
hard on myself as a kid
I believed everything
was my fault.

Correspond with yourself across time.

First, write a letter to your present-day self from your childhood self. In it, confess those things you felt guilty about that were not under your control.

Next, write back to your childhood self from your present-day self, explaining the reasons why you were not at fault for what happened.

"It is in pardoning
that we are pardoned."
Saint Francis of Assisi

In the form of scripted dialogue, tell a person (real or fictional) how grateful you are for a dramatic change you've made in your life. Have them respond in the way you think they would.

What would they say? How would they act?

Then have them respond in the way you think they *should.*

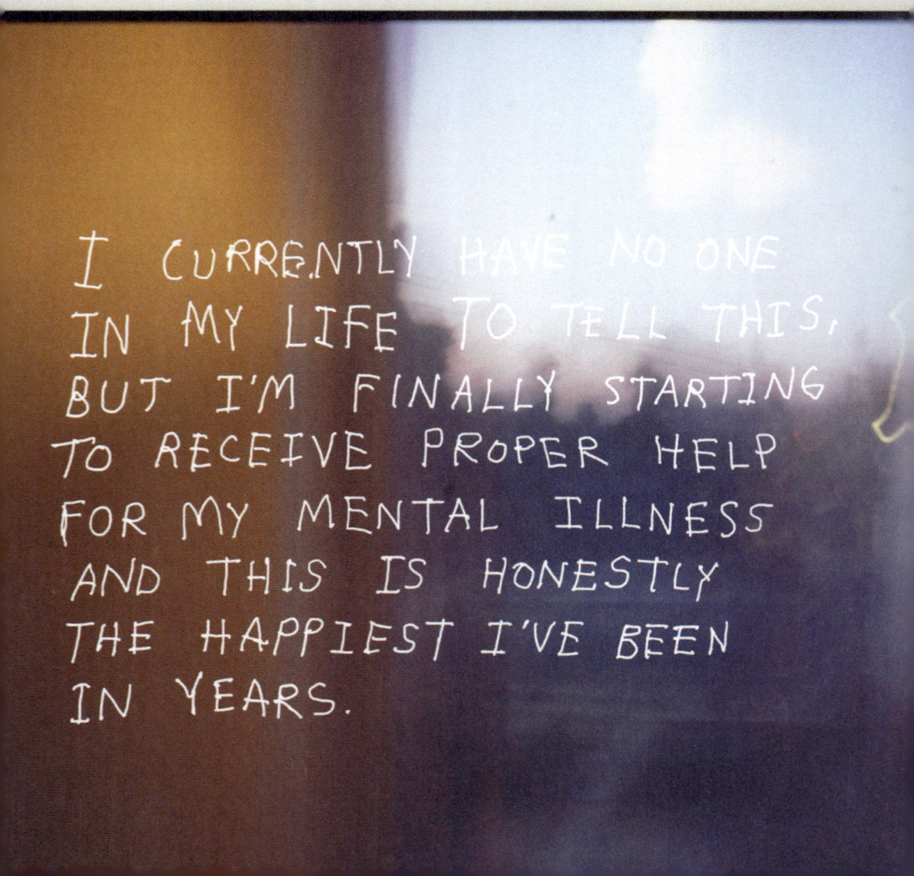

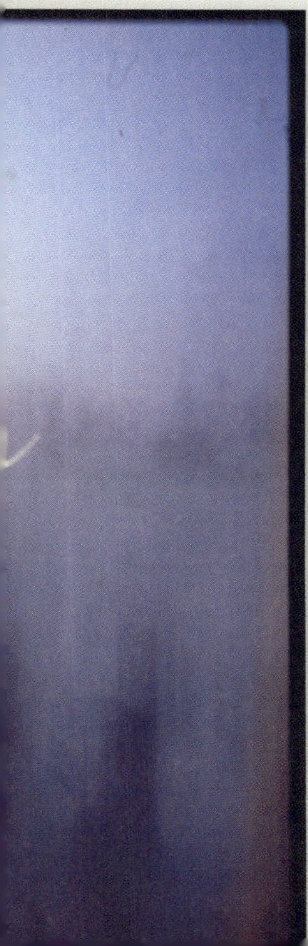

"For the Present is the
point at which time
touches eternity."
C. S. Lewis

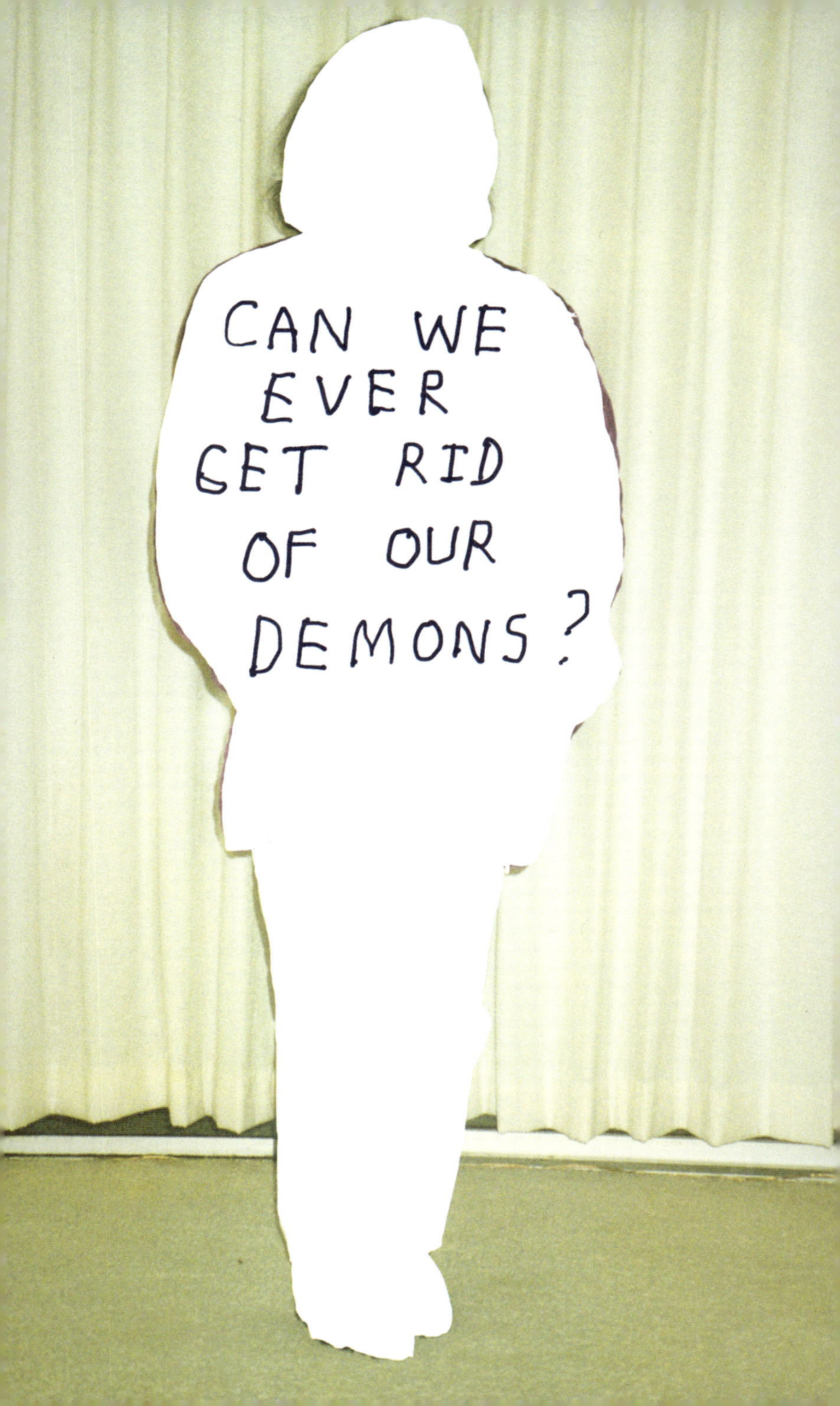
CAN WE
EVER
GET RID
OF OUR
DEMONS?

In his epic poem *The Divine Comedy*, Dante Alighieri journeys through inferno, or hell, depicted as nine different circles of increasing torment. He uses this as an allegory to represent the journey of the soul toward God.

In order to slay your personal demons, travel through your own version of hell. Name the nine different circles, and describe your journey—either in words or illustrations—toward what you consider to be salvation.

"From there we came outside and saw the stars."
Dante Alighieri

Compose a love poem—to yourself! Don't blush; you know you're the one you've always wanted to woo. Now you have official permission.

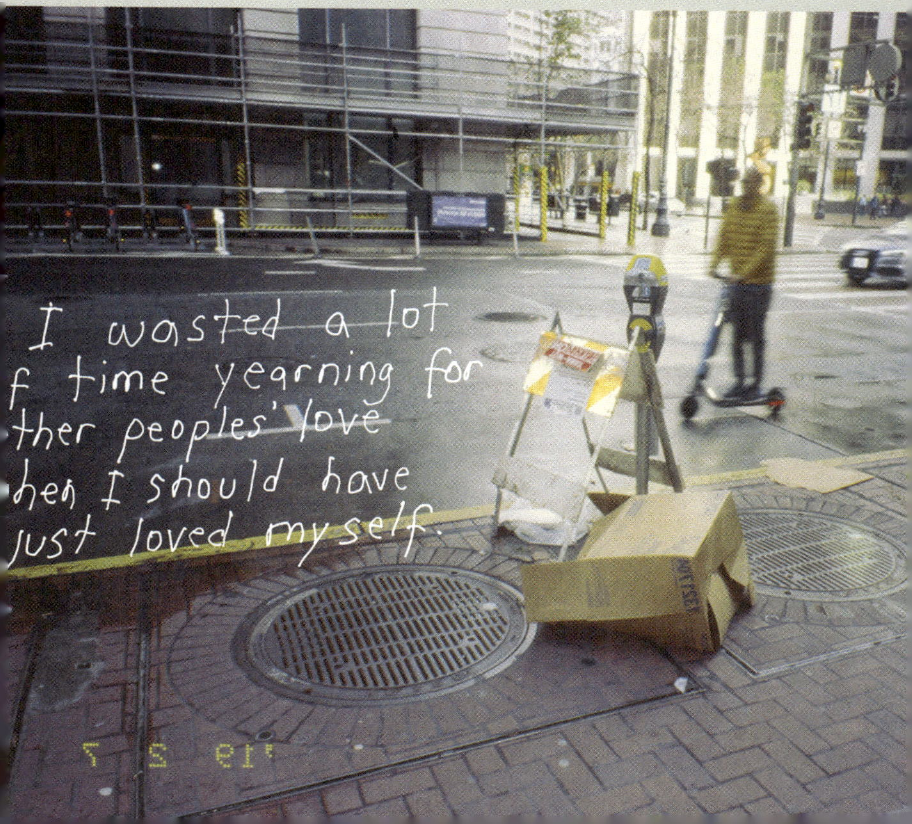
I wasted a lot
f time yearning for
ther peoples' love
hen I should have
just loved myself.

"Those who have courage
to love should have
courage to suffer."
Anthony Trollope

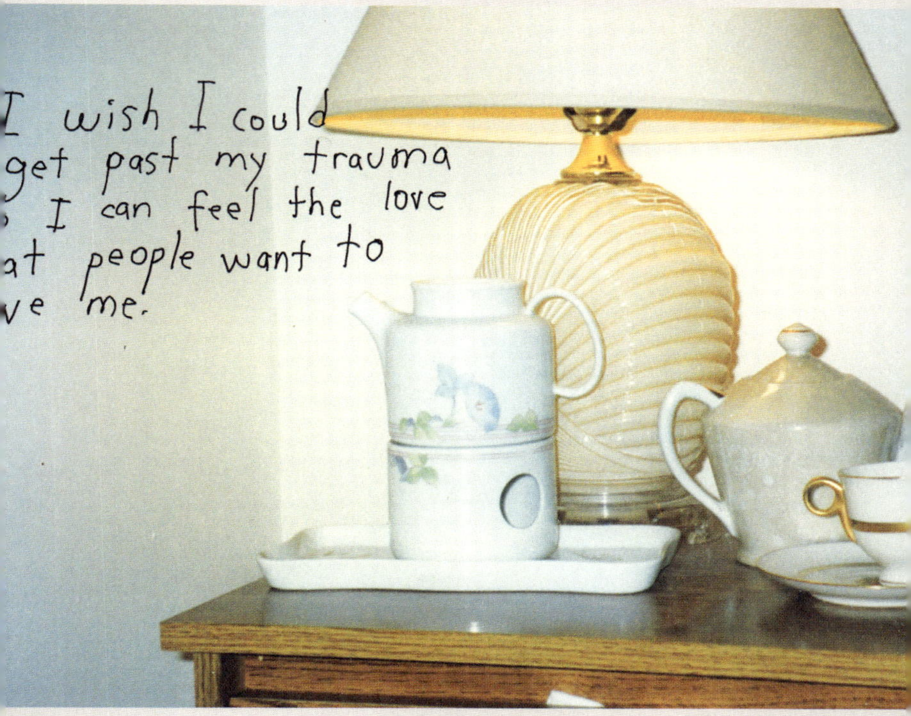
I wish I could
get past my trauma
I can feel the love
at people want to
ve me.

Sometimes the key to overcoming laziness when you know your body is craving movement is to just lace up a pair of sneakers and get going. It's a simple first step to kick-start a journey that's good for you in the long run.

Now, give your emotions the same treatment.

Imagine you're writing an illustrated instructional manual that will provide step-by-step directions for moving past feelings of sadness, anger, or other emotions that are keeping you at a standstill and preventing you from moving forward. Write those steps and take the first one.

"The best and most beautiful things in the world cannot be seen or even touched. They must be felt with the heart."

Helen Keller

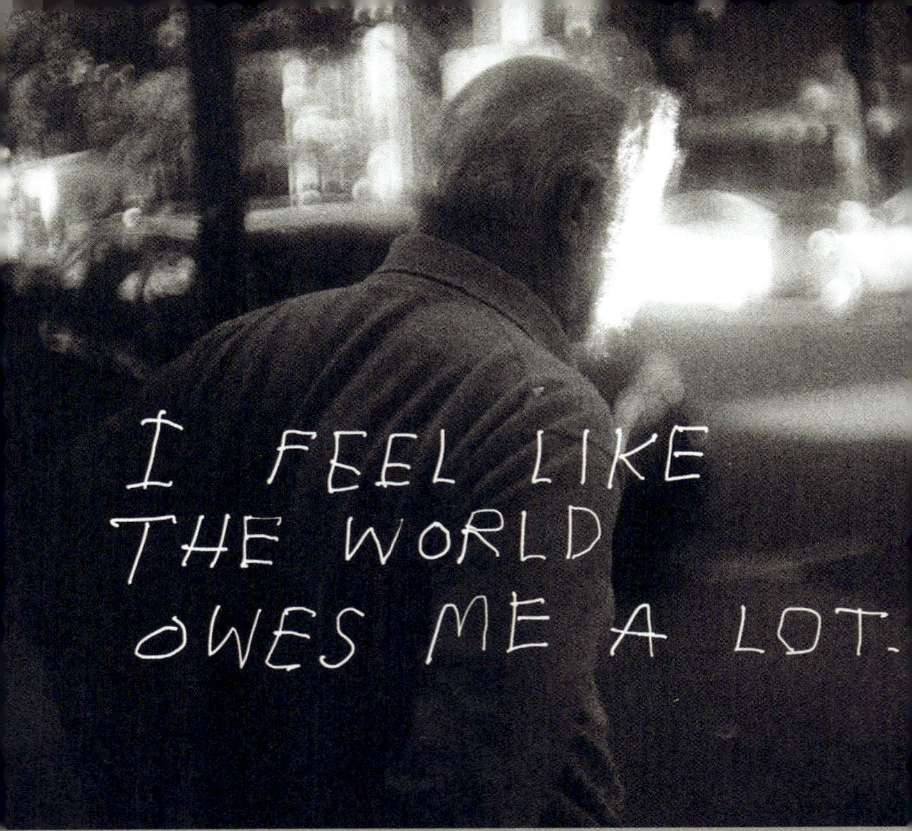

There are always going to be circumstances we can't control. We can either focus on what we think stands in our way, or we can evaluate our situation with honesty and distinguish what we have the power to change.

Create three lists. In the first, write the things you desire or want to achieve. In the second, write any factors you feel are preventing you from reaching each of those goals. In the third, write some small steps you can take to change or improve the circumstances that stand between you and your dreams.

In spite of difficulties, does focusing on what you have the power to change instead of the things standing in your way make the life you want feel more within reach?

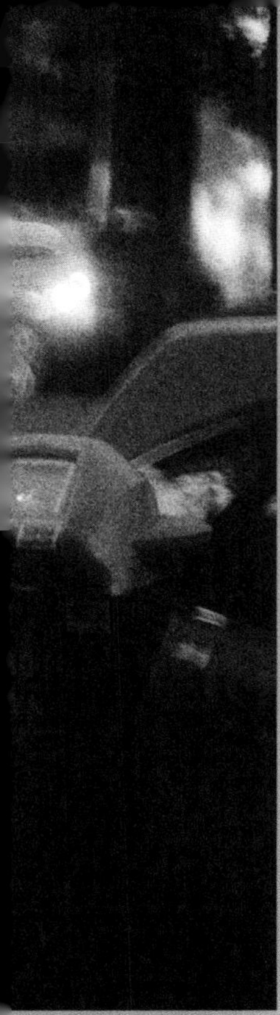

"If you have built castles in the air, your work need not be lost; that is where they should be. Now put the foundations under them."

Henry David Thoreau

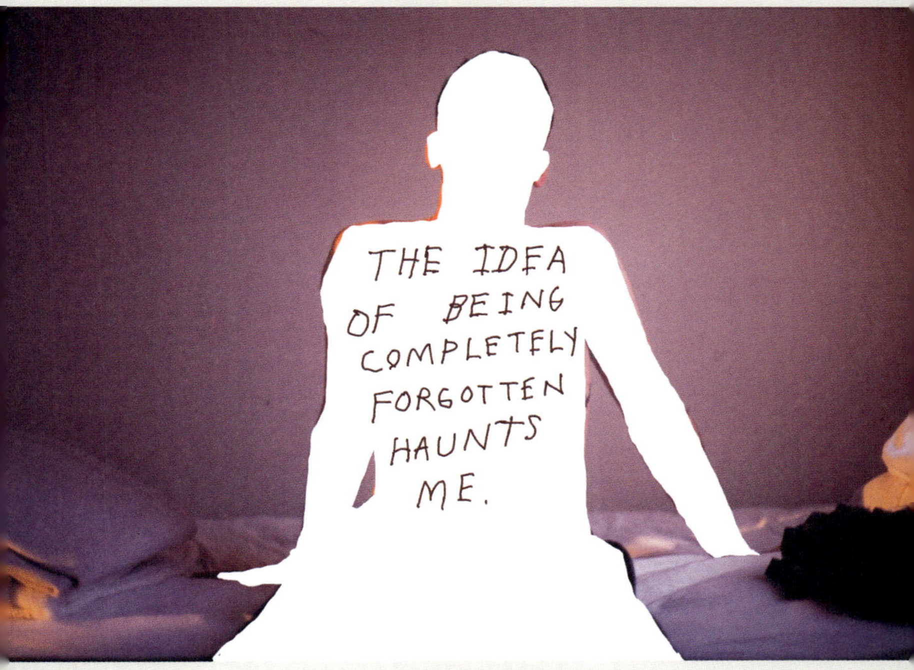
THE IDEA
OF BEING
COMPLETELY
FORGOTTEN
HAUNTS
ME.

It's the year 2100. You are a ghost. Instead of being haunted, you're now the one doing the haunting. A remembrance ceremony is taking place. A speech is being given. It's about you! Who's giving the tribute? In their voice, write your commemoration.

"My humanity is
bound up in yours,
for we can only be
human together."
Desmond Tutu

Any achievement can sometimes feel like a little death. It's human nature to long for things, so when that goal is no longer on the horizon, what will you aim for?

It's easy to name material goals—a job, a place to live, or accrued wealth—but what about achievements in character? What kind of person do you hope to be? Generous? Intelligent? Peaceful? Adventurous?

Think about who you want to be five years from now. What are three small things you can do today to begin becoming that person?

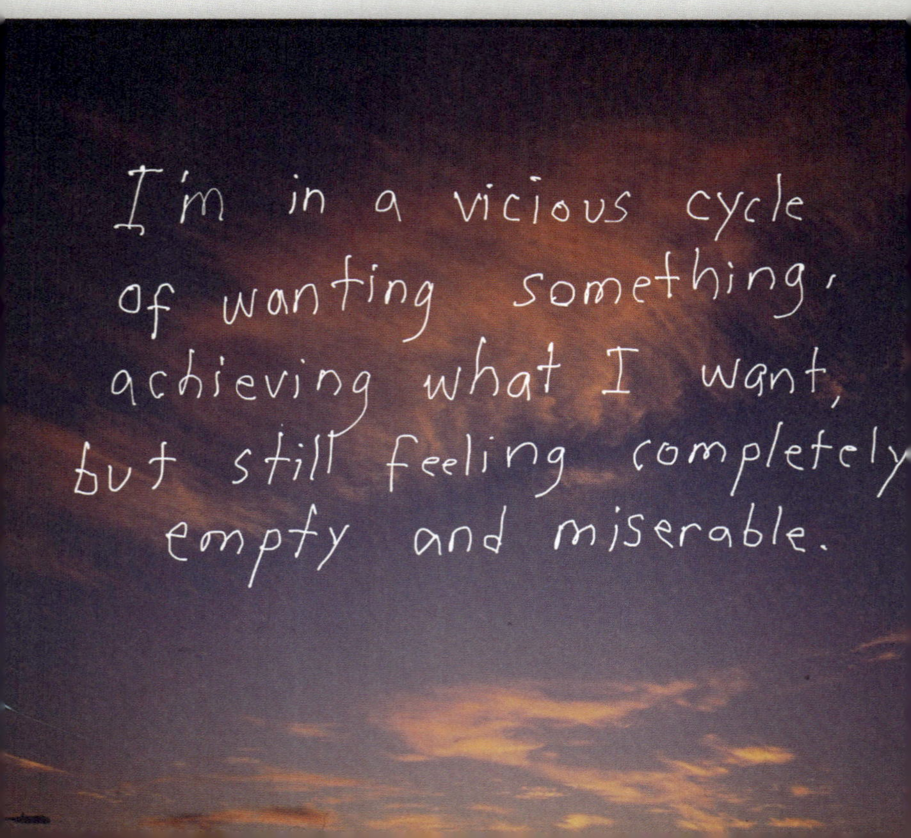

"Only those who
attempt the absurd
can achieve the
impossible."
Albert Einstein

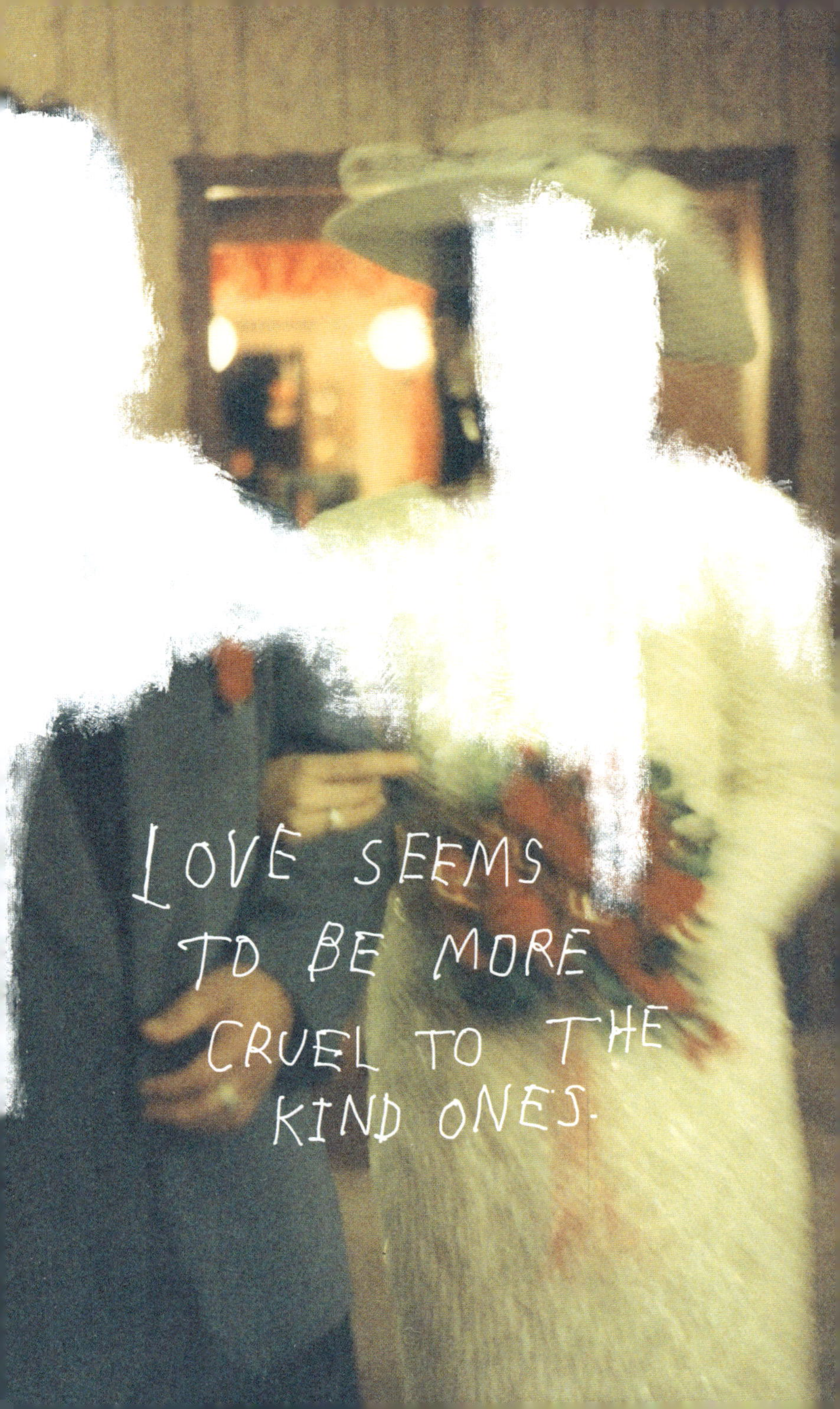
LOVE SEEMS
TO BE MORE
CRUEL TO THE
KIND ONES.

Is love crueler to the kind ones? Or is it that the cruel ones are less able to feel love?

"One is loved because one is loved. No reason is needed for loving."

Paulo Coehlo

Put yourself inside the shoes of a person who has offered you forgiveness or charity that you felt you didn't deserve. Write a letter to yourself from their perspective.

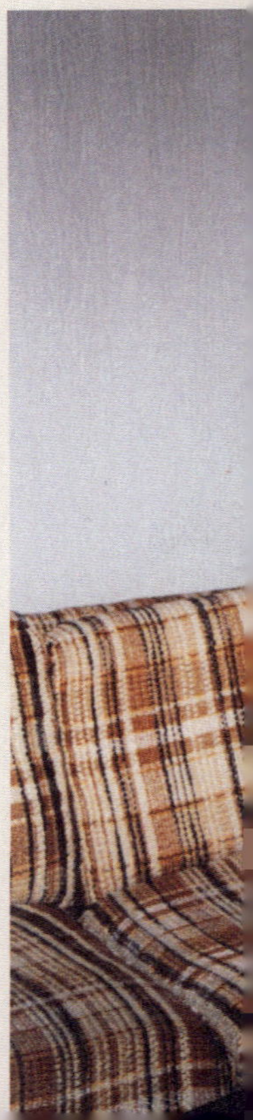

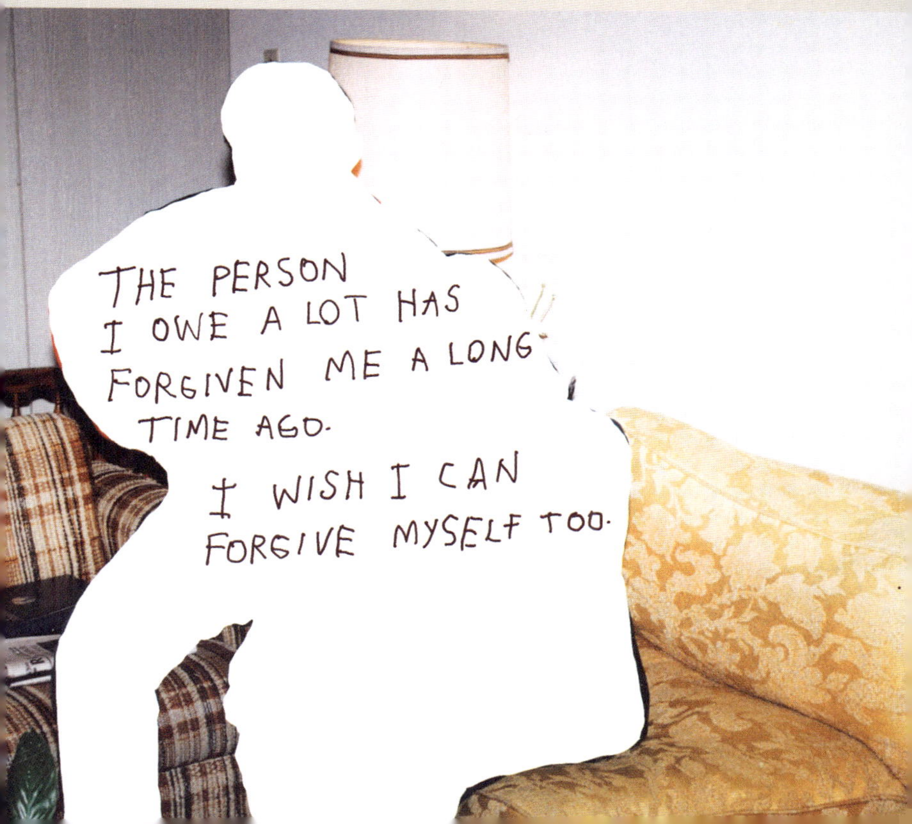

THE PERSON
I OWE A LOT HAS
FORGIVEN ME A LONG
TIME AGO.
I WISH I CAN
FORGIVE MYSELF TOO.

"Forgiveness is
the fragrance that
the violet sheds
on the heel that
has crushed it."

Mark Twain

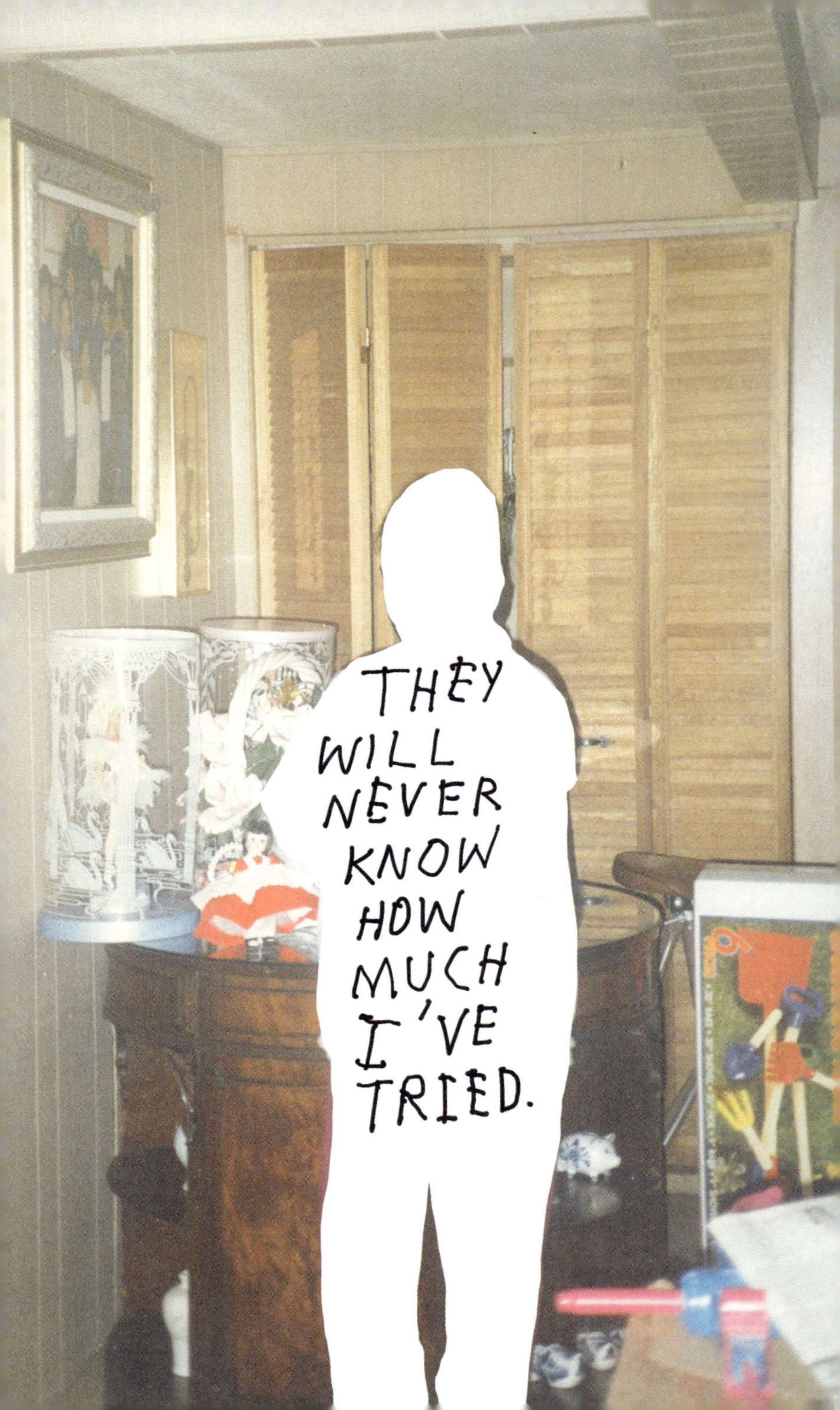
THEY
WILL
NEVER
KNOW
HOW
MUCH
I'VE
TRIED.

It's 1983, the height of the graffiti era in New York City. You're in a subway station and have five minutes before the next train arrives. In that time, color the wall with as many tags as you can that will tell the arriving passengers the story of your life.

Ready, set . . .

"I never paint dreams or nightmares. I paint my own reality."

Frida Kahlo

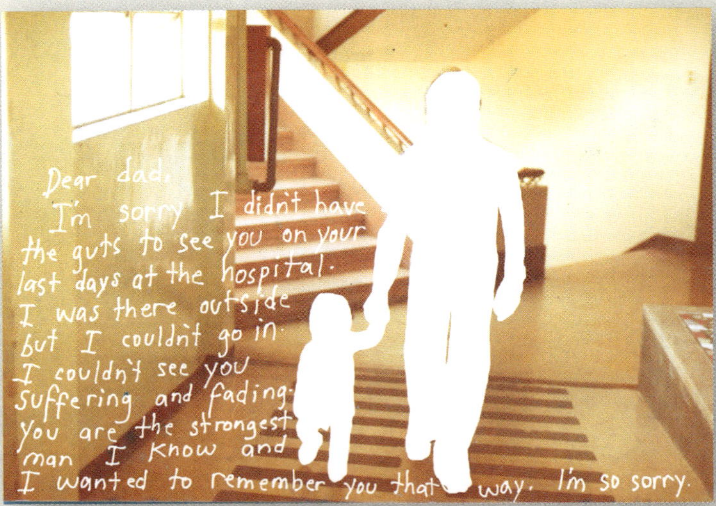

Write a letter to someone you've loved and lost. Explain something you regret not doing for them while they were alive.

"Maybe all one can do is hope to end up with the right regrets."

Arthur Miller

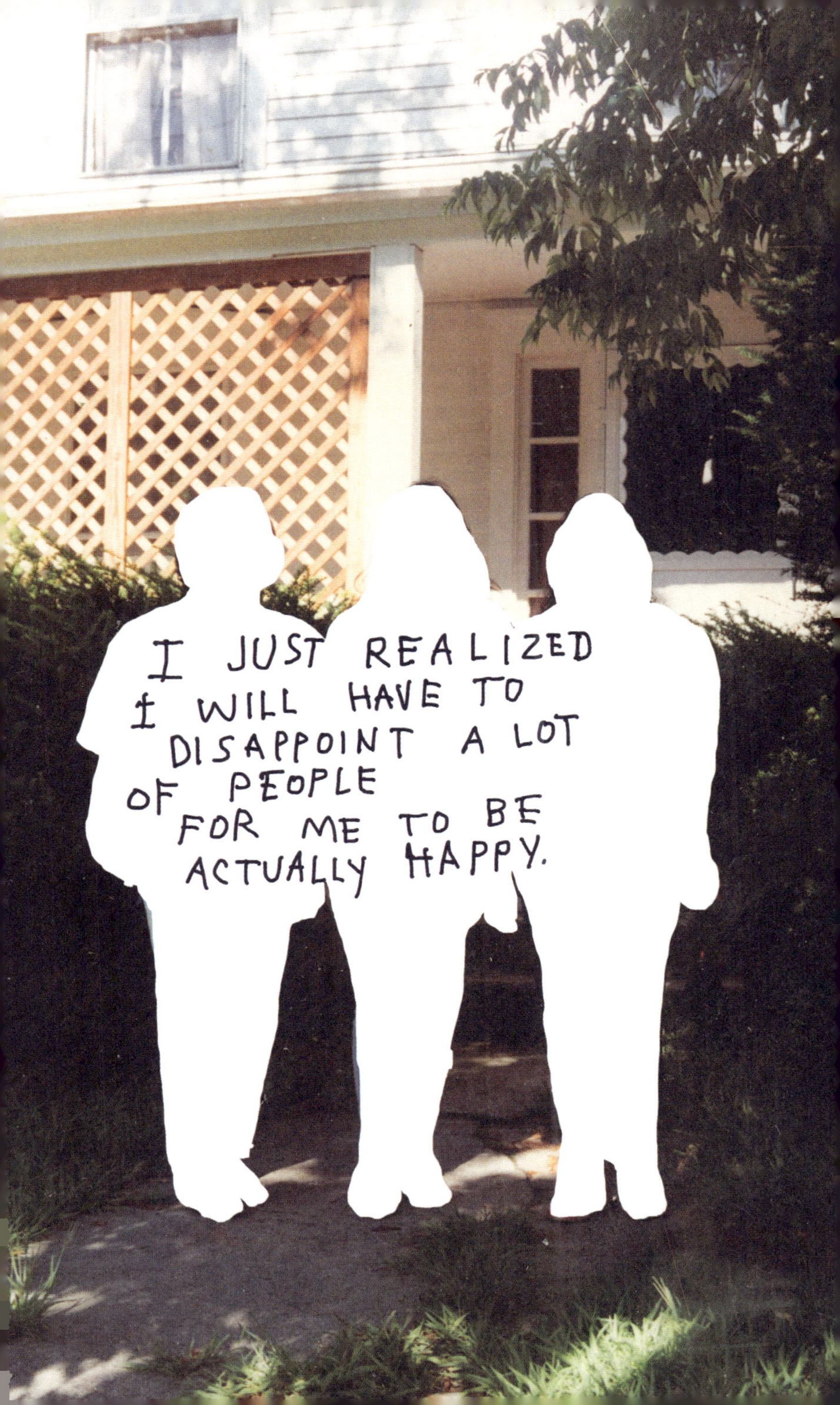
I JUST REALIZED
I WILL HAVE TO
DISAPPOINT A LOT
OF PEOPLE
FOR ME TO BE
ACTUALLY HAPPY.

Consider whether if, by disappointing people now, the happiness you derive from staying true to yourself might lead to their satisfaction with you later.

"To be yourself in a world that is constantly trying to make you something else is the greatest accomplishment."
Ralph Waldo Emerson

You've taken someone who has hurt you to a secret court. The only people who will ever know about the trial are the judge and jury. You are the prosecutor of your own case. Write out your closing argument and ask for the punishment you think the defendant deserves.

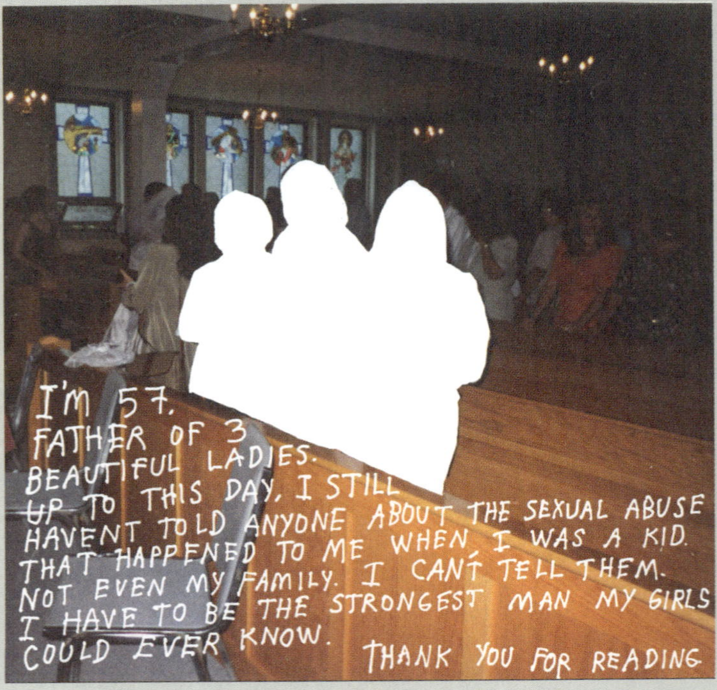

"It is better
to risk saving
a guilty person
than to condemn
an innocent one."
Voltaire

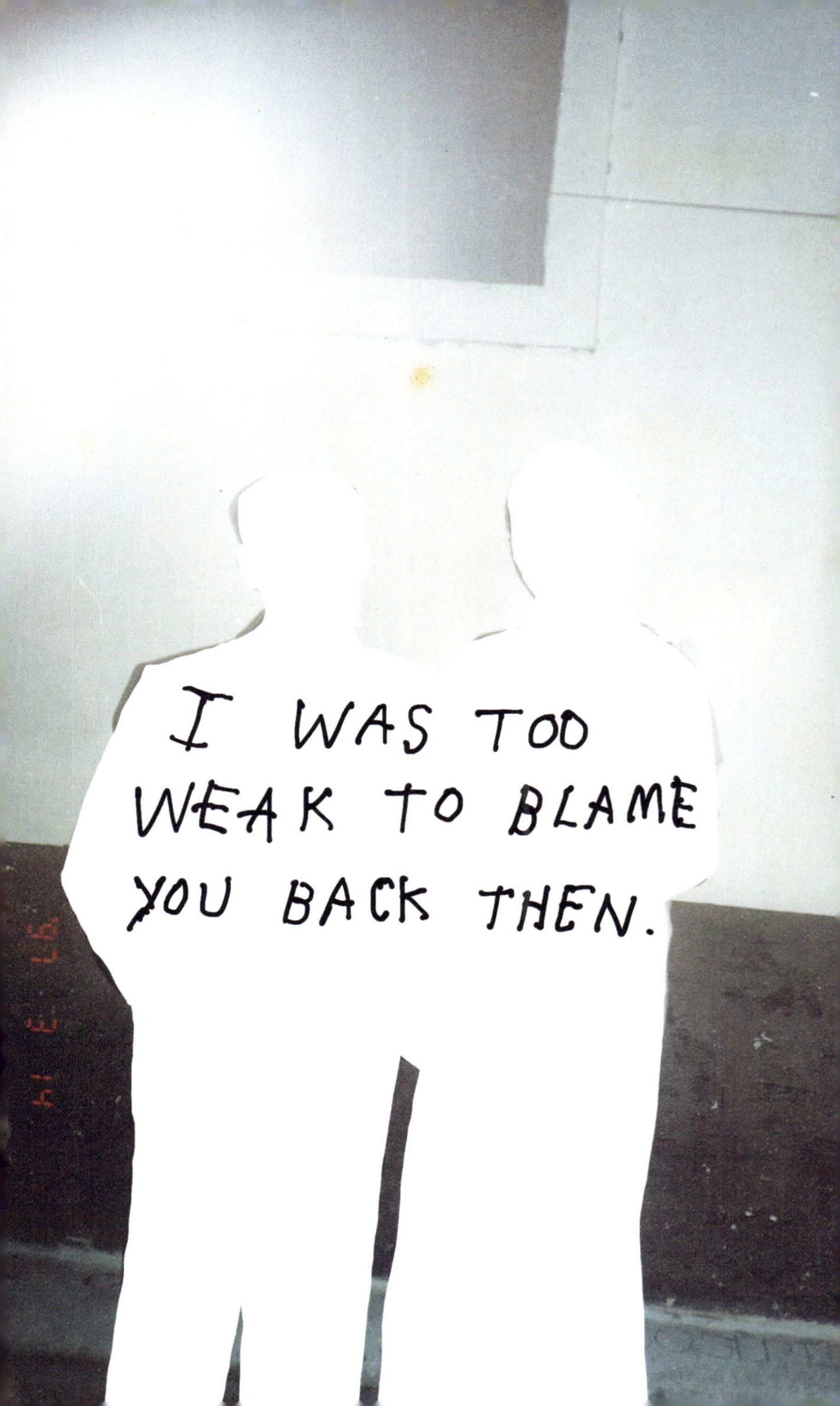
I WAS TOO
WEAK TO BLAME
YOU BACK THEN.

J'accuse! Time to serve up some blame.

First, write an accusatory letter to a person who wronged you in the past. Then, write an accusatory letter to the person they might have become. How do they differ? Which version of the person are you able to forgive more easily?

"The weak can never forgive. Forgiveness is the attribute of the strong."

Mahatma Gandhi

We can learn a lot about ourselves from listening to conversations between strangers. Spend an entire day eavesdropping on the overheard dialogues around you, and determine what you can infer about the people speaking.

Who is insecure? Prideful? Imaginative? Funny?

Now consider how your spoken words communicate your inner character to the world. Is the picture you paint of your inner world accurate?

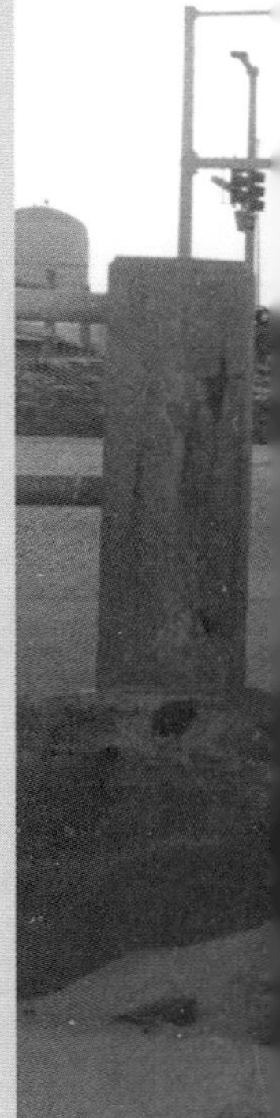

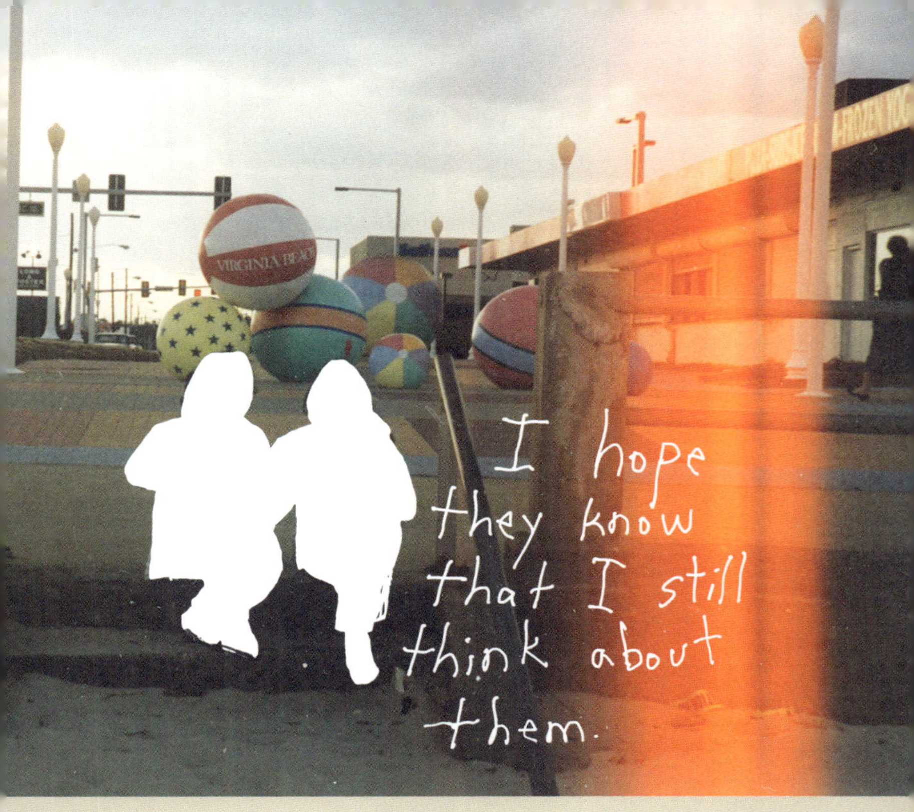
VIRGINIA BEACH
I hope they know that I still think about them.

"She had become really quite expert, she thought, at listening as though she didn't listen, at sitting in other people's lives just for a minute while they talked round her."

Katherine Mansfield

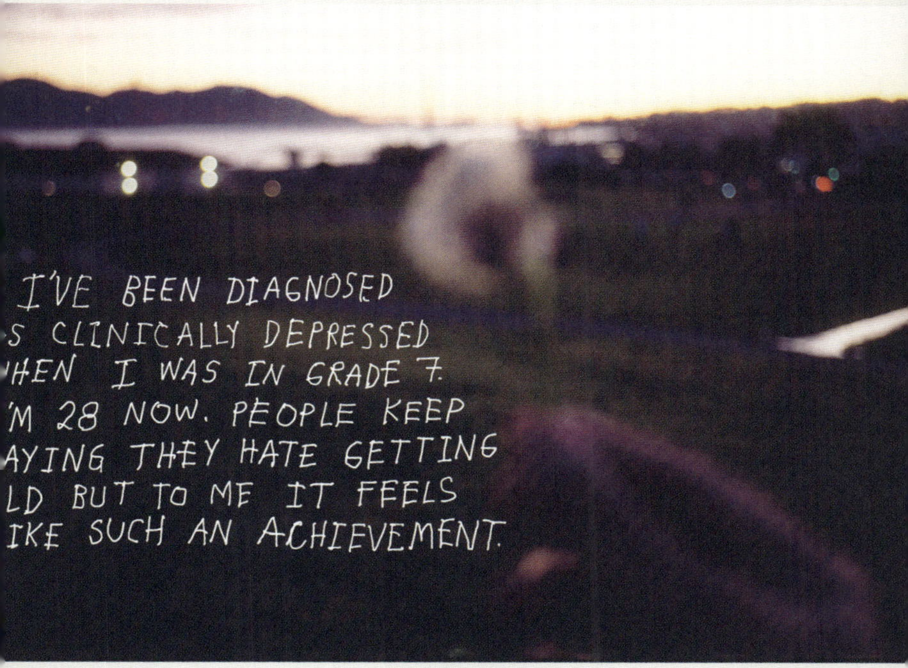
I'VE BEEN DIAGNOSED
S CLINICALLY DEPRESSED
HEN I WAS IN GRADE 7.
'M 28 NOW. PEOPLE KEEP
AYING THEY HATE GETTING
LD BUT TO ME IT FEELS
IKE SUCH AN ACHIEVEMENT.

DNA is not destiny. And neither is a diagnosis. Consider a disadvantage you've overcome. How has that experience given you a perspective that differs from the people who have not endured the same?

"Suffering becomes beautiful when anyone bears great calamities with cheerfulness, not through insensibility but through greatness of mind."
Aristotle

What do you hope to create before you die? Is it a physical thing? The fulfillment of an idea? Is it tied to relationships with family, friends, or community? Are you trying to fulfill someone else's idea of success? If so, maybe it's time to envision what success means to *you*.

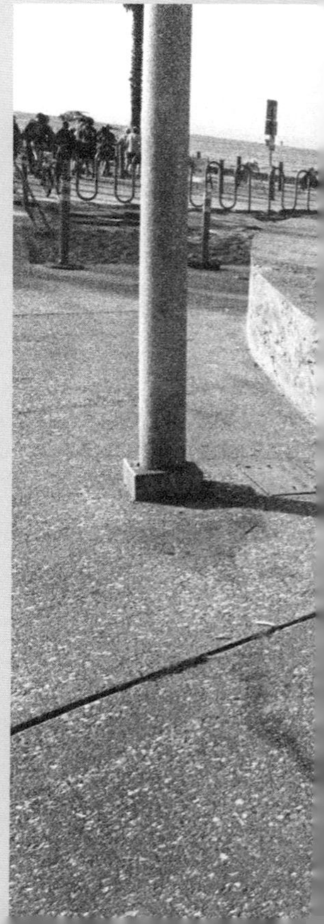

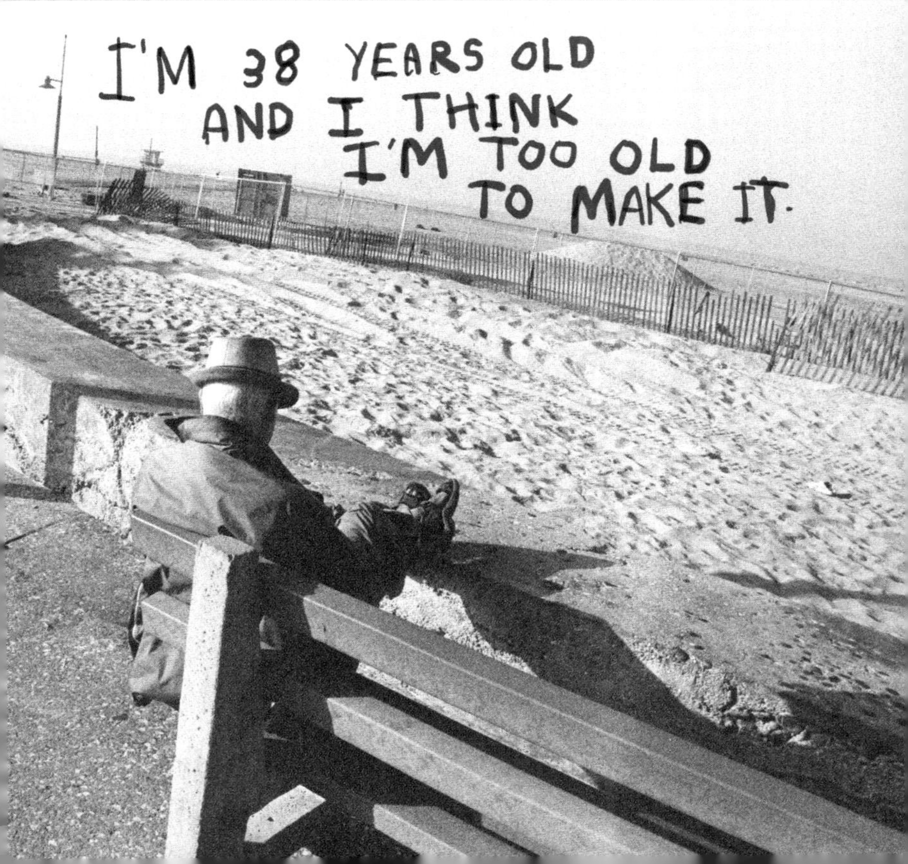
I'M 38 YEARS OLD
AND I THINK
I'M TOO OLD
TO MAKE IT.

"Don't wait for the
right opportunity:
create it."
George Bernard Shaw

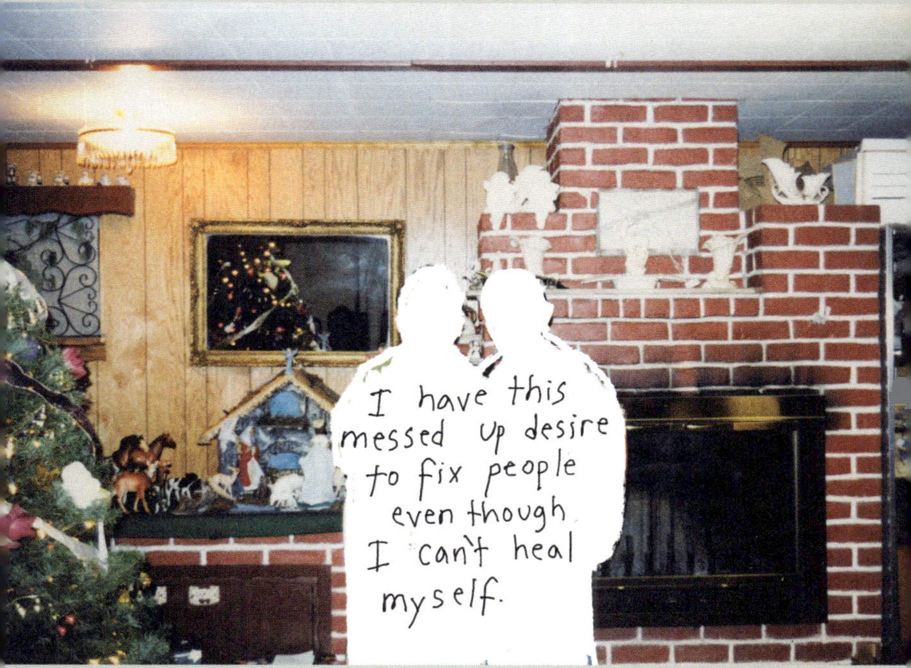
I have this
messed up desire
to fix people
even though
I can't heal
myself.

Physician, heal thyself" (Luke 4:23 KJV). In biblical times, this proverb was used to express the belief that before a doctor could cure others, they must first treat themselves. It's often easier to see the flaws in other people and remain blind to our own.

Make a list of the bad (or even just annoying) qualities you've observed in the people who populate your life, present-day or in the past. Now, examine whether you embody any of these things yourself. Does admitting you're guilty of some of these shortcomings allow you to have more grace for others?

"We all are men,
in our own natures
frail, and capable
of our flesh; few
are angels."

William Shakespeare

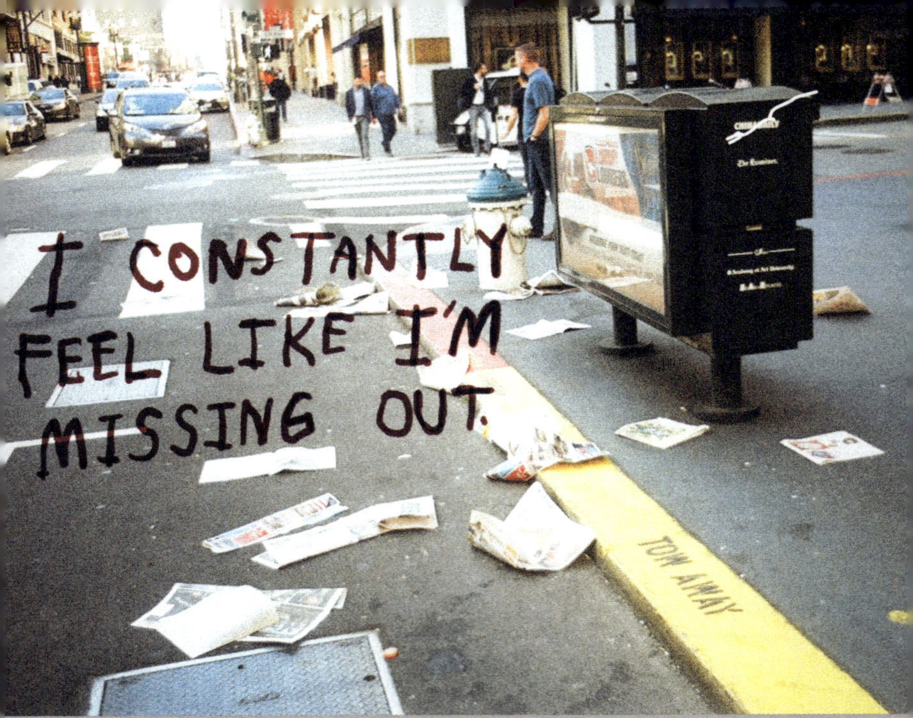

FOMO, also known as the "Fear of Missing Out," can almost always be solved by going out and getting some FROYO, also known as frozen yogurt.

What kind of FOMO do you suffer from, and which flavor of FROYO would help to get rid of it?

"That fear of
missing out on
things makes
you miss out on
everything."
Etty Hillesum

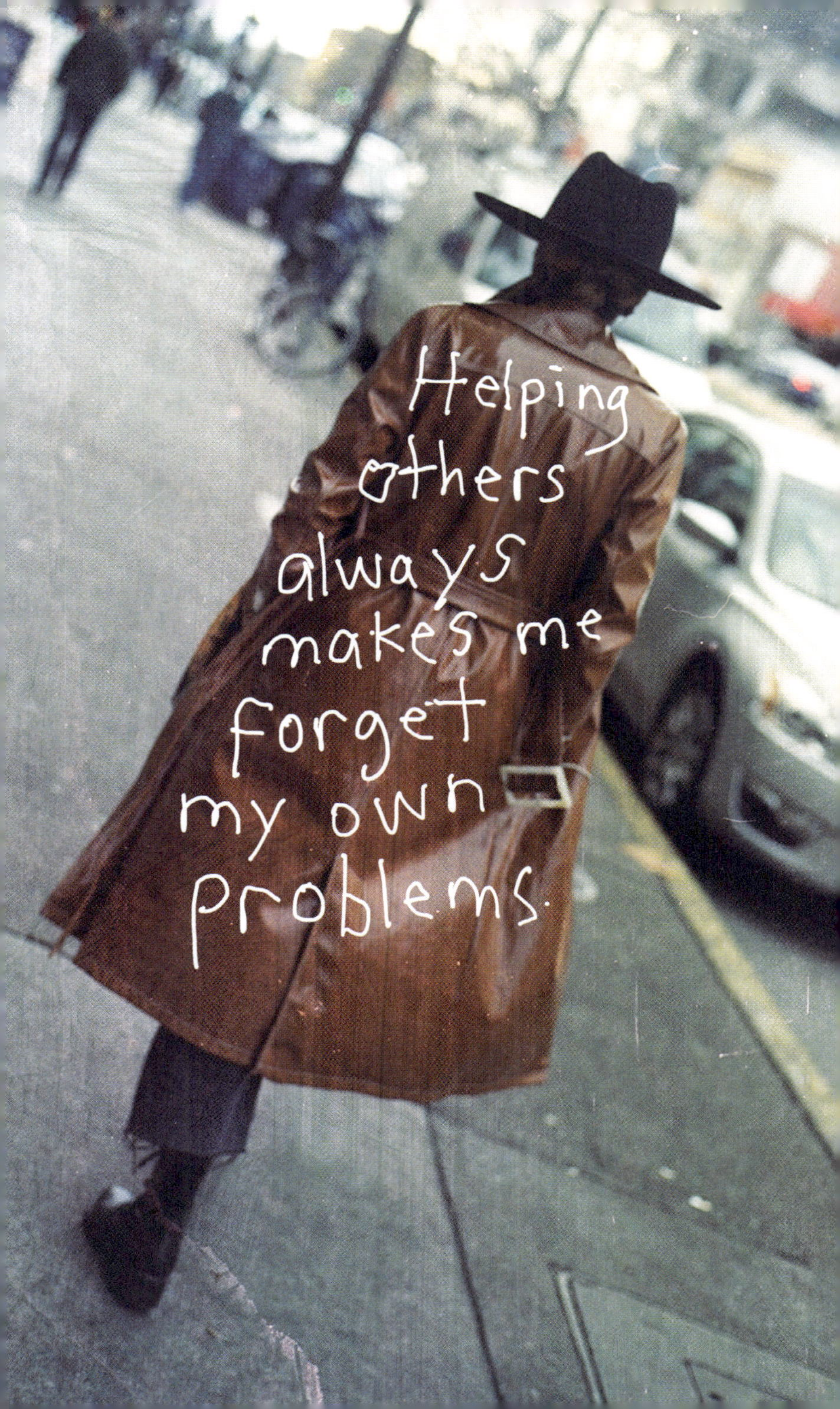
Helping others always makes me forget my own problems.

Bruce Wayne transforms into the vigilante superhero Batman in part to overcome memories of the violent murder of his parents when he was a child. Create an original alter ego for yourself. Whom would they focus on helping? What memory are they attempting to escape?

"No one is
useless in
this world
who lightens
the burdens
of another."
Charles Dickens

Día de los Muertos—the Day of the Dead—is an annual holiday that originated in Mexico, during which people come together to honor the dead with food, drinks, parties, and activities that their lost loves ones enjoyed during their lives. Rather than a spirit of mourning and sadness, it's a holiday marked by lively celebrations and joy, a testament to the gift of life.

If you woke up this morning with air in your lungs, you've been given a gift. How will you spend the day celebrating the things you love most?

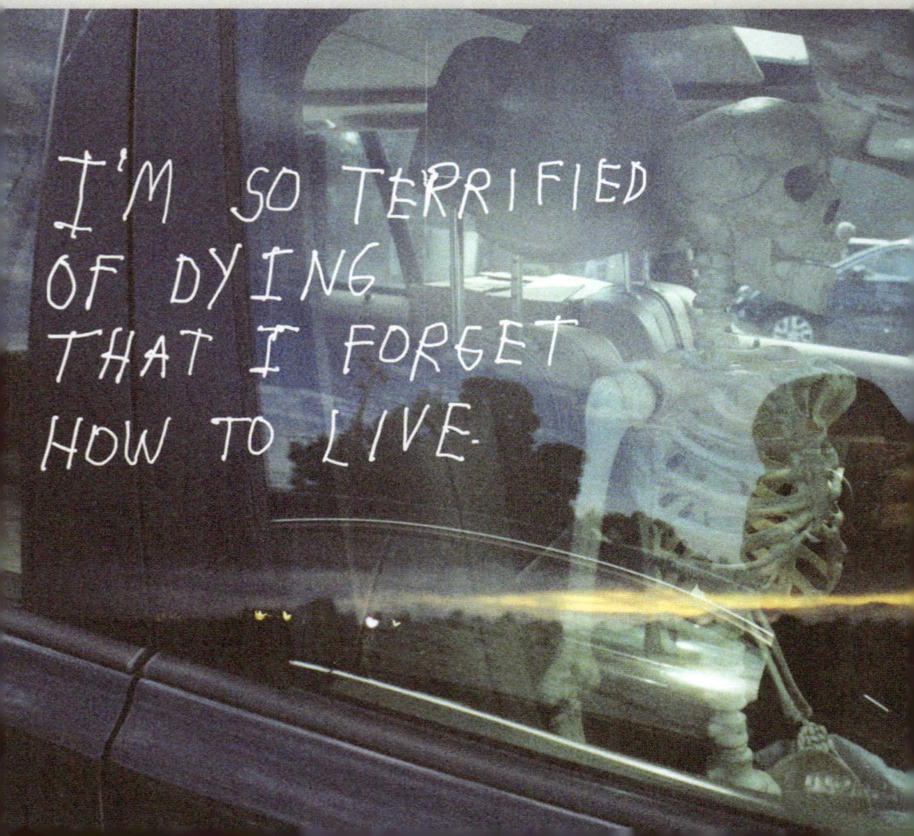

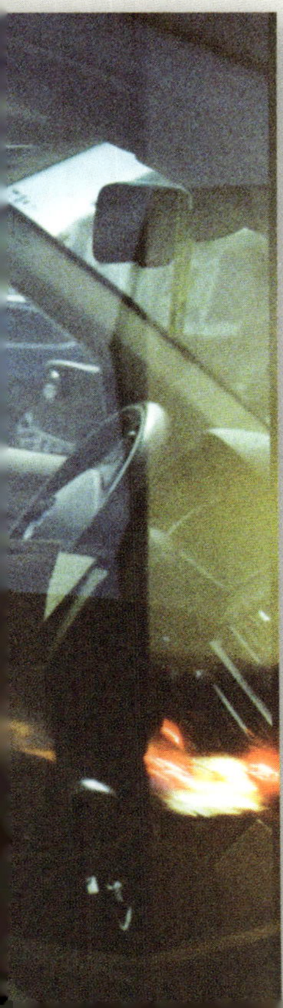

"The way to love
anything is to
realize that it
may be lost."

G. K. Chesterton

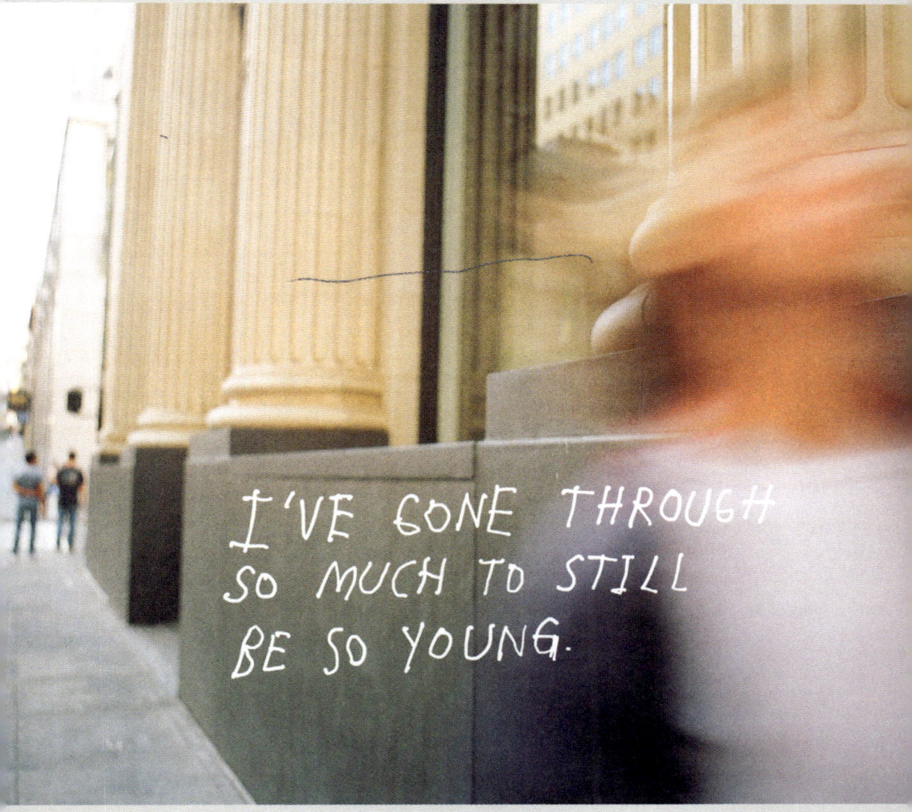
I'VE GONE THROUGH
SO MUCH TO STILL
BE SO YOUNG.

A **re you an old soul** or young at heart?

"I don't believe in
aging. I believe in
forever altering
one's aspect
to the sun."
Virginia Woolf

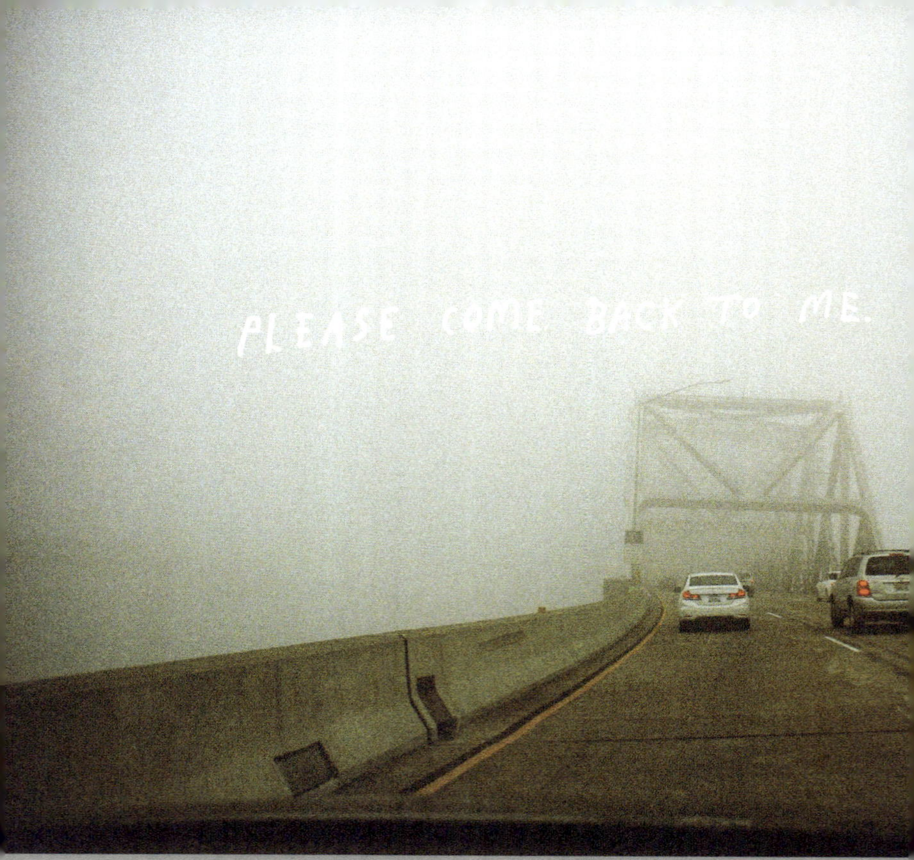

But if I do, *then where will we go?*

Have you ever parted ways with someone and then attempted to reunite with them? It's never like it once was. Describe an experience when you made the right decision, but then went back on it for the sake of familiarity or comfort.

"I could have not
returned, and
I've returned."
Gabriela Mistral

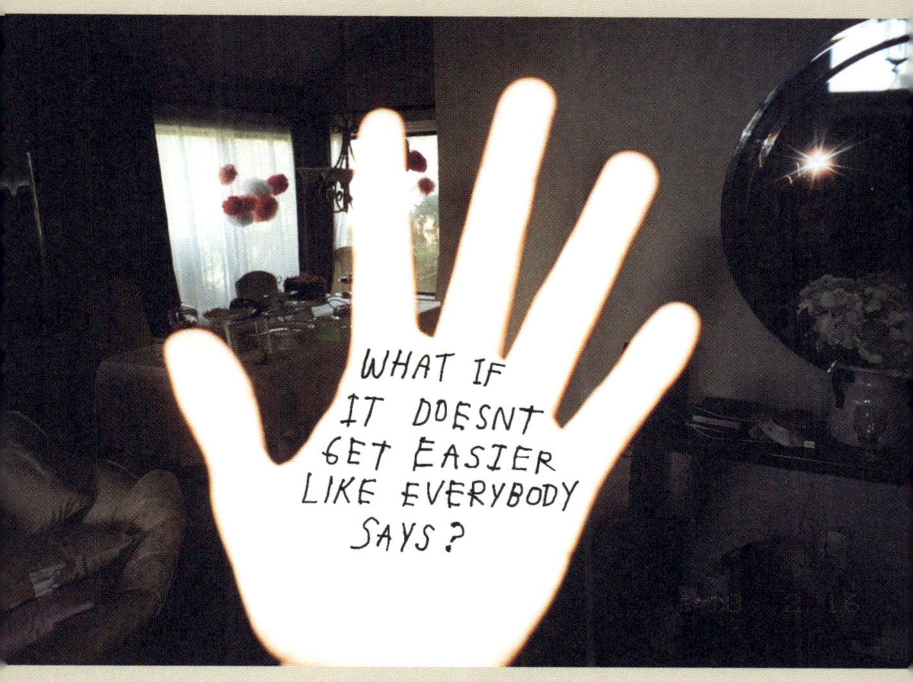
WHAT IF
IT DOESNT
GET EASIER
LIKE EVERYBODY
SAYS?

What if you wrote down your ten biggest fears for the future? And then let them go?

What **if** . . . what **if** . . . what **if** . . . ?

"Man is not worried by real problems so much as by his imagined anxieties about real problems."

Epictetus

Would da Vinci's *Mona Lisa* still be a masterpiece had it never been hung in a museum? Is there something or someone in your life others might see as unremarkable, but you see as extraordinary?

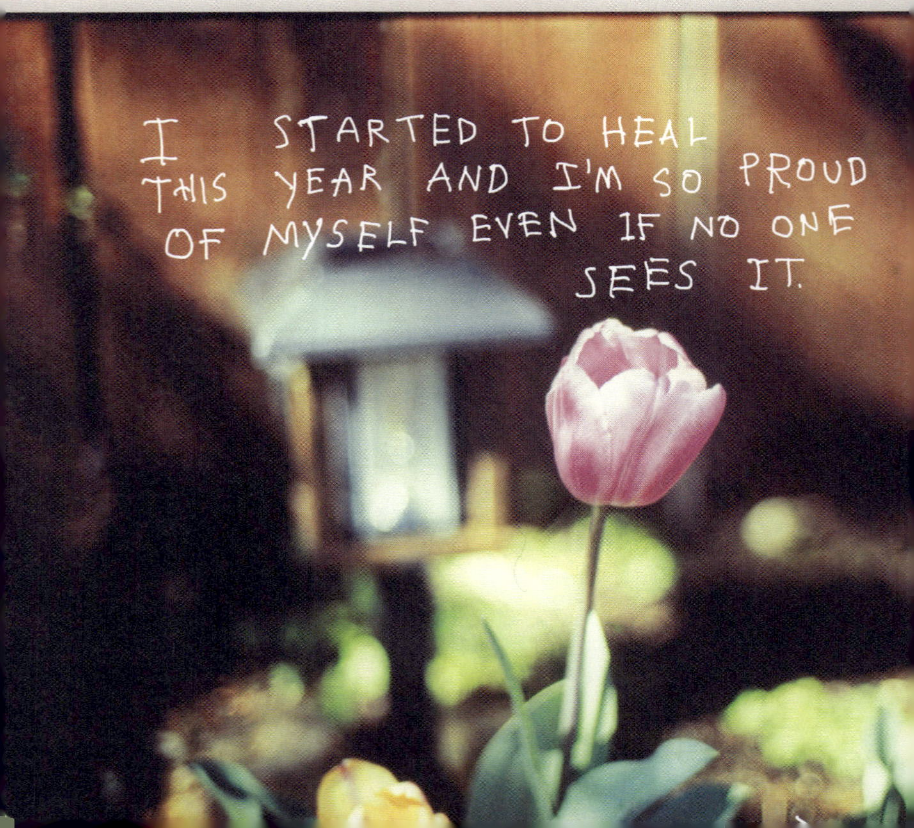

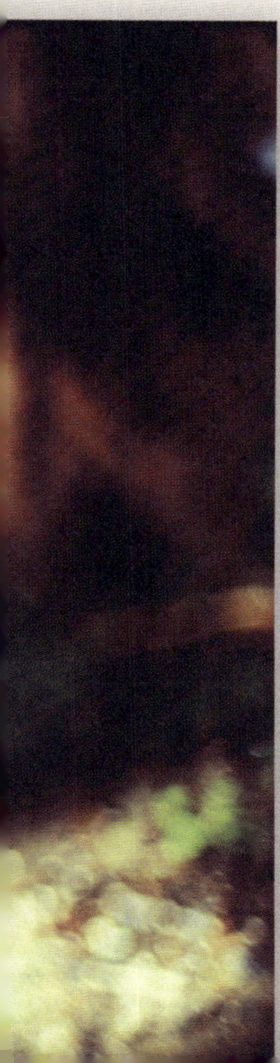

"Nothing can be loved
or hated unless it is
first understood."
Leonardo da Vinci

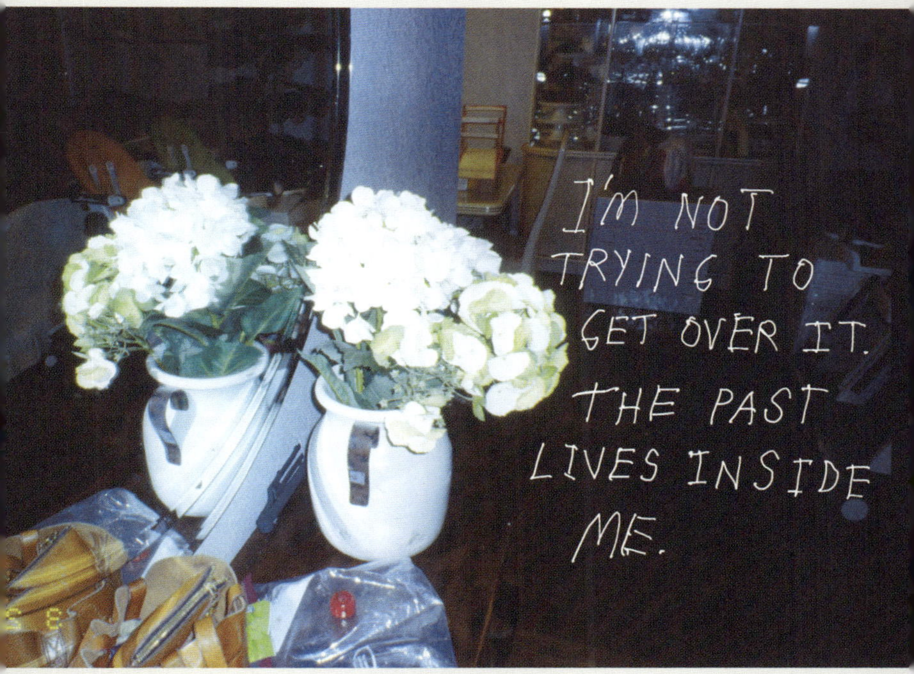
I'M NOT
TRYING TO
GET OVER IT.
THE PAST
LIVES INSIDE
ME.

Every hero's journey begins with a call to adventure. It disrupts the comfort of the ordinary world and presents a challenge or quest that must be undertaken.

You are the hero in the story of your life. Rather than letting the events of your past define you, consider the notion that whatever happened to you before is just the beginning of your journey.

Where will you go from here?

"If you follow someone else's way, you are not going to realize your potential."

Joseph Campbell

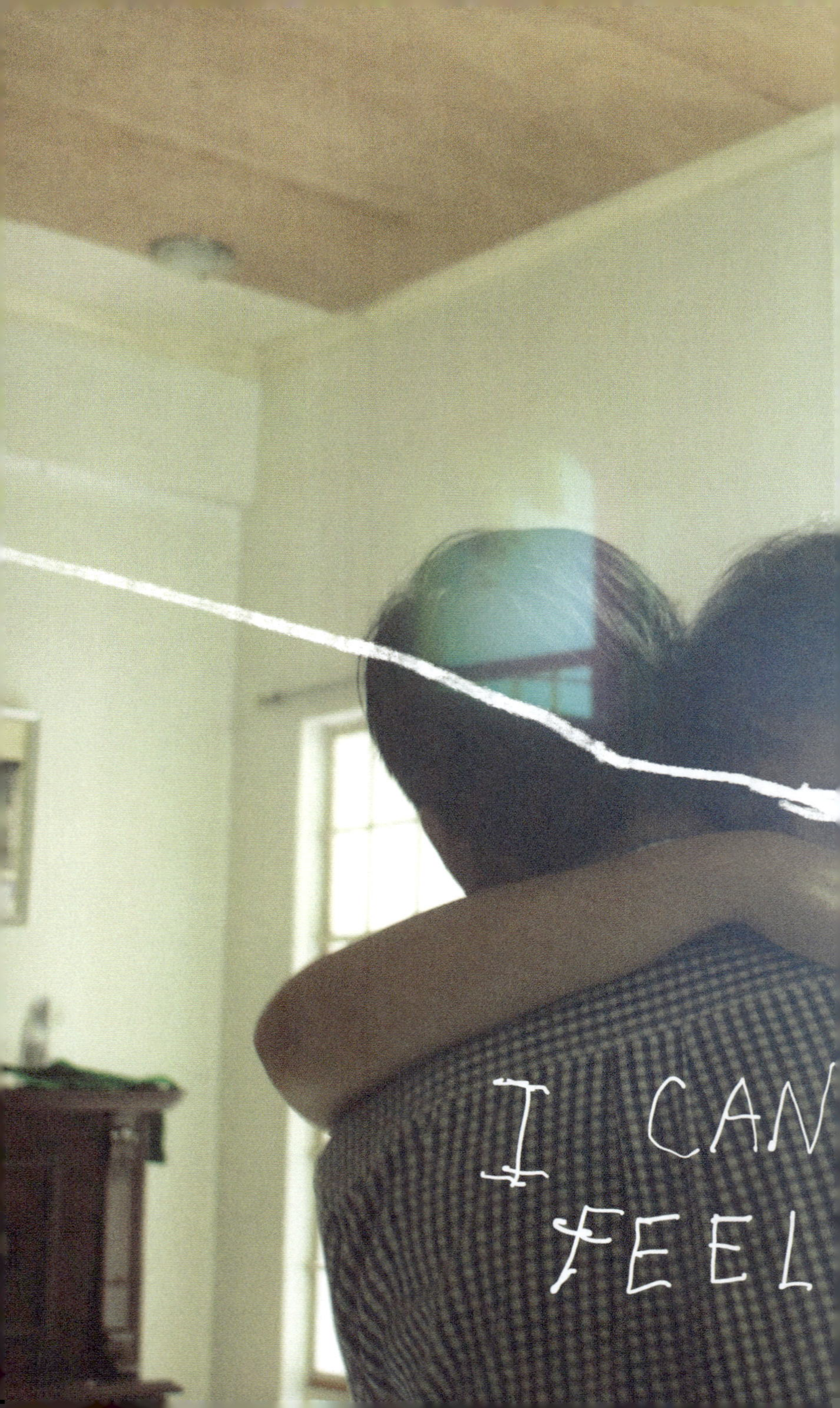
I CAN
FEEL

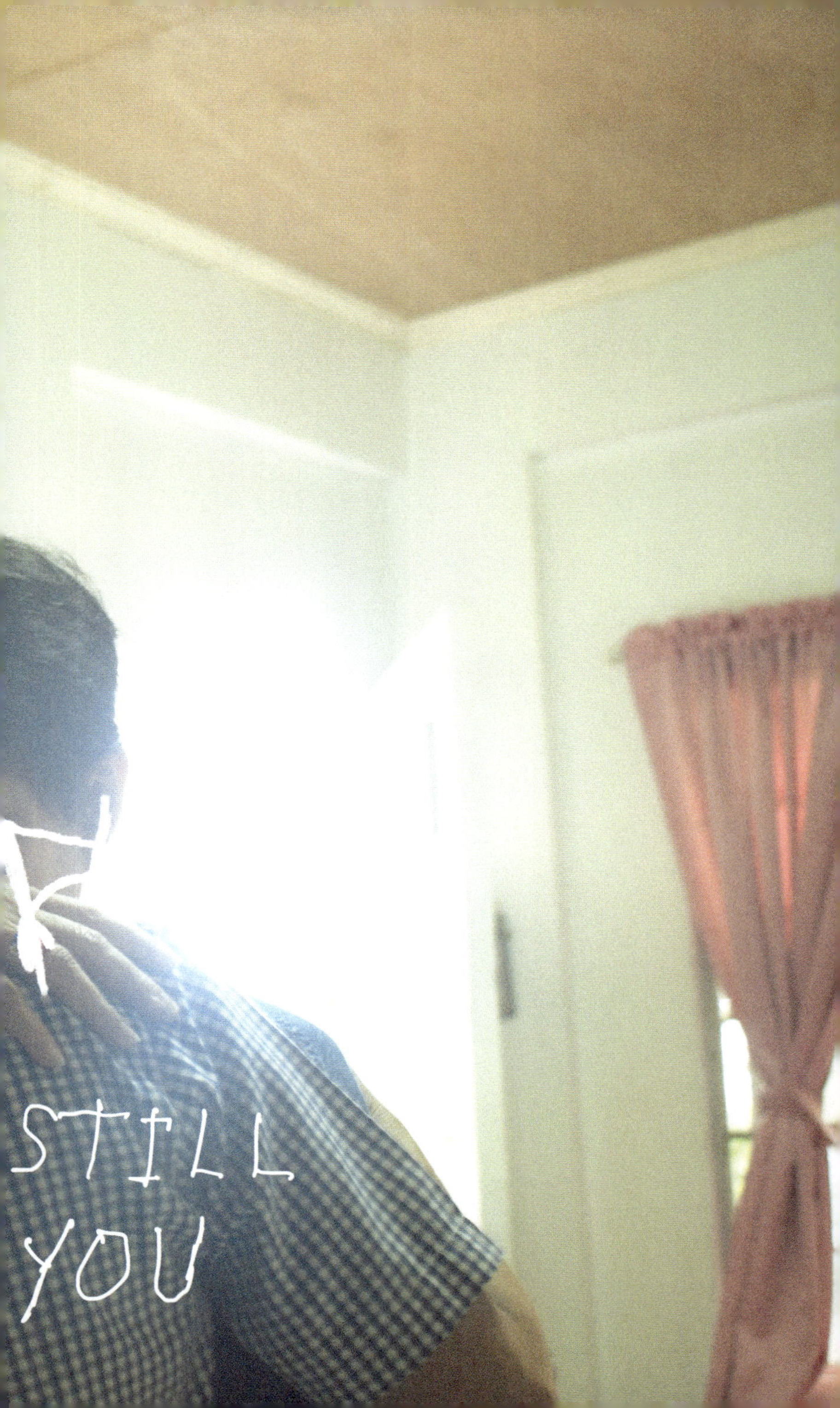
STILL
YOU

ACKNOWLEDGMENTS

While the project "Things you wanted to say but never did" is a collaboration of strangers, as the one who started it, it wouldn't have been made without my struggles as an immigrant. For that, I am acknowledging all the immigrants around the globe who left their homes to take a chance at a better life.

My families.

My family in the Philippines, my foundation, who supported me all the way. Benjie, Nognog, Badet, and Cring. I owe my life to you. Thank you.

My family in the USA, who made sure we had a roof above our heads, food on our table, and clothes to keep us warm. Choly, Tony, Patrick, Hershe, Anthony, James, and Gail, thank you for making me feel like I never left home.

My Liberty and Narra. My core group. My purpose.

My wife, Liberty, who believed in me and trusted my own pacing and timing. My confidant, my critic, my fan, and my partner for life.

My daughter, Narra, who always makes sure I'm okay. Thank you for the songs, the kisses, and the hugs. You can read this by the time this goes out. Please know that you are the greatest gift to me. I love you.

My best friends, Geric, Roemart, and Kookoo.

My dearly departed friends, Xavier and Toby.

Friends I've not met or have yet to meet. All the strangers who shared their stories, who supported the project and my other works. I will forever be thankful to all of you.

And lastly, this book wouldn't be possible without the contributions of all these people from Harper Celebrate: Michael, Kathleen, Bonnie, Marilyn, Tiffany, Robin, Stephanie, and Yaniv. Thank you for being with me on this journey.

MARAMING SALAMAT.

"I take pictures.

I draw.

I listen."

—GELOY CONCEPCION

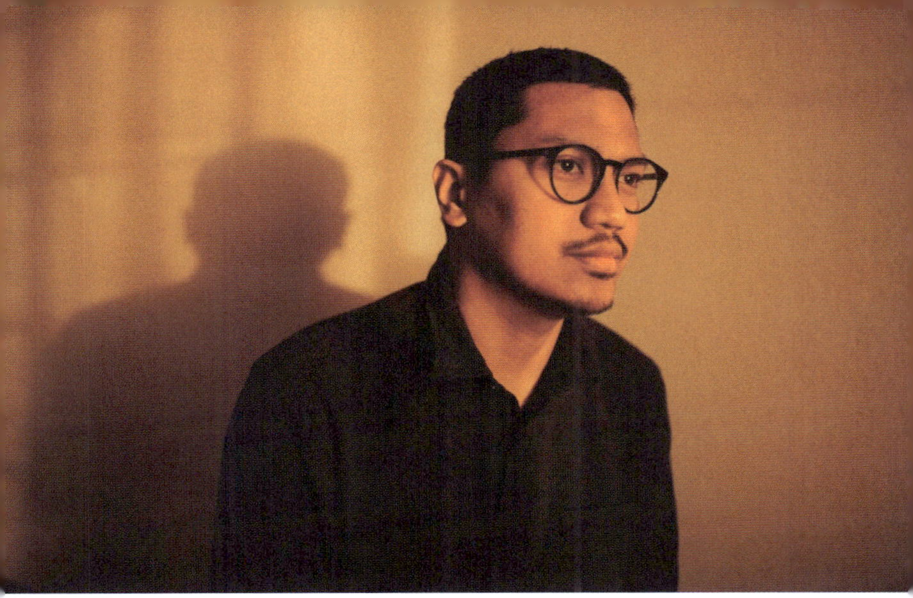

ABOUT THE AUTHOR

Geloy Concepcion finished his degree in Advertising at the University of Santo Tomas College of Fine Arts and Design. He started joining exhibitions in 2011 and has exhibited his work in the Philippines, Cambodia, Taiwan, Singapore, India, and the Netherlands. He was an artist-in-residence at Casa San Miguel in Zambales from 2012 to 2013 and was a member of Pilipinas Street Plan. His work was included in the 2016 Pride Photo Awards and the 2017 Human Rights Arts and Film Festival. His ever-changing approach to photography is intertwined with his personal journey. His current photographic works stem from experimentation in portraiture, drawing, street art, and life as a migrant Filipino in the US.

#thingsyouwantedtosaybutneverdid

instagram.com/geloyconcepcion